THE SPEECH, AND ITS CONTEXT:

JACOB BLAUSTEIN'S SPEECH "THE MEANING OF PALESTINE PARTITION TO AMERICAN JEWS"

GIVEN TO THE BALTIMORE CHAPTER, AMERICAN JEWISH COMMITTEE

FEBRUARY 15, 1948

BY

ABBA A. SOLOMON

Copyright © 2011 Abba A. Solomon
All rights reserved.

ISBN 978-1-257-01073-8

Inquiries:

TheSpeech.and.ItsContext@gmail.com

KEY TO CITATIONS

AJC   Library and Archives of the American Jewish Committee, New York City.
ajcarchives.org   Searchable on-line database of digitized records of the organization. Citation includes the file name of the group of documents in which record is found.
AJHS   American Jewish Historical Society, Newton Centre, Mass. and New York, N.Y.
AJYB   *American Jewish Year Book.*
FRUS   *Foreign Relations of the United States.*
JHU   The Collected Personal and Business Papers of Louis and Jacob Blaustein, MS 400, Special Collections, Milton S. Eisenhower Library, The Johns Hopkins University, Baltimore, Maryland.
NYPL   The New York Public Library.
PRO FO   Public Records Office, Foreign Office records, London, UK.
YIVO   Records of the American Jewish Committee (AJC) deposited in care of the YIVO Institute for Jewish Research, Center for Jewish History, New York City.

Undated cover photograph of Jacob Blaustein speaking, and photographs on pages 184 and 189, used by permission from the Collected Personal and Business Papers of Louis and Jacob Blaustein, MS 400, Special Collections, Milton S. Eisenhower Library, The Johns Hopkins University.

The so-called Jewish State is not to be called by that name but will bear some appropriate geographical designation. It will be Jewish only in the sense that the Jews will form a majority of the population.

American Jewish Committee
President Joseph Proskauer, Sept. 15, 1946[1]

We would be saying we were misled (-not that I disagree with telling that if we finally fail in correcting the situation).

American Jewish Committee
President Jacob Blaustein, October 12, 1949[2]

---

1 Proskauer to Executive Board, Sept. 15, 1946. See page 95.
2 Blaustein to Proskauer, letter, Oct. 12, 1949. See page 180.

Acknowledgments

I would not have been able to accomplish this book without the excellent assistance of the library professionals **Cynthia Requardt**(retired), **Margaret Burri**, **Kelly Spring**, and **Jim Stimpert**, at Special Collections, Milton S. Eisenhower Library, The Johns Hopkins University, Baltimore, Maryland, entrusted with the care and presentation of the Collected Personal and Business Papers of Louis and Jacob Blaustein.

The generous cooperation and liberal openness of **David Singer**, Director of Research at the American Jewish Committee, New York City, is a tribute to that organization.

Michele Anish, who during my research was Librarian of the Blaustein Library and Archives of the American Jewish Committee, saved me innumerable hours by her willingness to share her knowledge of the Committee's records of over 100 years of service to Jews and gentiles in the United States and around the world.

The Center for Jewish History, the home of **YIVO Institute for Jewish Research** and the New York location of the **American Jewish Historical Society**, is a New York City custodian of Jewish archival material which is supportive and welcoming to researchers. The Center also houses the Leo Baeck Institute, the American Sephardi Federation, and Yeshiva University Museum.

Permissions to reproduce the material in this book and the extensive professional help I have received from these institutions of knowledge, is gratefully acknowledged. Of course, responsibility for the use to which the material is turned is mine alone.

Abba A. Solomon

My special thanks to Abraham Raher and Eleanor Solomon of Baltimore, for facilitating my work there, and to my dear Yehudit, Judith E. Solomon, without whom this book would not exist.

Contents

The Significance of Jacob Blaustein's Speech, and its Historical Context 1
    Ambiguity and Clarity..4
    Jewish Violence and the Urgency for Partition...................6
    The AJC's Public Posture..9
    1948 — The State of Israel is Declared............................11
    The Mission of the AJC —
    Understanding its Support for Israel...............................14

Jacob Blaustein to the Baltimore Chapter,
American Jewish Committee, February 15, 1948............................17

I. The American Jewish Committee,
the Zionist Organization
& the Balfour Declaration..49
    "Much enthusiasm among our down-town co-religionists."............51
    Before Balfour / Ottoman Palestine.................................54
    "The general impression appears to be that the Shomerim are
    innocent of aggression."...57
    A Conference or a Congress?..59
    "The American Jews stand united"..................................63
    "We cannot blink the fact nor leave the whole subject to the
    Zionists."..67
    The AJC Statement: "A Weak Straddle"?..........................70
    "Upbuilding" Palestine—Forming the Jewish Agency............73
    Interpreting Balfour...80
    "Zionism is but an incidence of a far-reaching plan."............83
    "We need work of a patient, simple kind."........................85
    "The American blow will be more painful."......................89

II. The AJC until Palestine Partition..91
    "Beyond any consideration of good or evil."......................93
    "This miasma of Jewish unity."....................................101
    "They are not our enemies."..103
    The AJC and Jews in the Arab Countries:
    "We consider the lives of the Jews of Yemen and of Egypt no less
    important than Jewish lives in Palestine."......................107

"No room can be made in Palestine for a second nation except by dislodging or exterminating." 109

"It was originally a straddling document, and its amendment would probably lead to additional straddling." 113

"The only difference between Judge Lazansky and myself is a matter of emphasis." 117

"We naturally move to those places where we are not persecuted, and there our presence produces persecution." 122

"The negation of Jewish life in the Galut...." 126

The Stern Memo: What Kind of State? — 1943 130

"Most of the Yishuv are absolutely blind to any possibility other than Jewish statehood." 134

III. The AJC after Declaration of the State of Israel 139

Blaustein — Man in the center 141

Advocacy for the New State 149

"Not only her own interests are involved, but those of the Jews in the United States and all over the world." 158

Qibya, 1953: "Adds one more ugly feature to an image already displeasing to many Americans." 161

Secret Peace Envoy to Egypt for Israel — 1954 169

A White House Visit — 1950 173

Restraining Nationalist Zionism: "Our Committee will be obliged to issue a severe, critical statement." 178

The Ben Gurion-Blaustein "Exchange of Views" — 1950 184

Identification with Zionism as Jewish Identity 190

"Well, it is probably the Indians." — May 1949 193

The AJC vs the ACJ 200

Index 205

The Significance of Jacob Blaustein's Speech, and its Historical Context

THE CORE of this book is a speech entitled "The Meaning of Palestine Partition for American Jews."

The book contains the full text of the February 15, 1948 address by American Jewish Committee (AJC) executive committee chairman (and next president) Jacob Blaustein to the Baltimore chapter of the AJC. The speech is found in the Collected Personal and Business Papers of Louis and Jacob Blaustein, at The Johns Hopkins University.[3]

Mr. Blaustein's speech is reproduced in pages 17-48. Added to the speech — as given — is text struck out from a February 8 draft version of the speech, found in the same folder in the Blaustein papers. That removed text, printed here in **bold** characters, seemed to this writer significantly different from the final presentation.

Following the speech, the book contains materials from the American Jewish Committee archives, the Blaustein papers at Johns Hopkins University, and other sources, which show the development of the AJC's policy relating to the Jewish "homeland" in Palestine, and the subsequent State of Israel.[4]

The genesis of this book was curiosity of this writer about the "Ben Gurion-Blaustein Statement" or "Exchange of Views" of 1950.

American Jewish Committee officers Joseph Proskauer and Jacob Blaustein objected to Israeli leaders stating or implying that Jews, especially Western youth, should return "home" to the new State of Israel. They insisted that Prime Minister David Ben Gurion (and subsequent Israeli PMs through Golda Meir) disavow statements that said or implied this, in a public "Exchange of Views" in Jerusalem, August 23, 1950.

In the exchange, Blaustein promised that the AJC and other American Jewish organizations, "within the framework of their American

---

3 The text used is from box 4.113, file VV-5-32, "Jacob Blaustein Speeches - AJC Ex Committee, Baltimore Chapter 2-15-48," JHU.
4 The AJC's newsletter, the *Committee Reporter*, said that in the "notable address...Mr. Blaustein called attention to the consistency and realism of the AJC's fundamental stand on Palestine since the issuance of the Balfour declaration in 1918..." "Partition Plan Linked to Peace," *The Committee Reporter*, vol. 5, no. 3, March 1948, page 1.

citizenship," would continue to "do all we can to increase further our share in the great historic task of helping Israel" — abandoning a threat to publicly split with the Zionist state.[5]

Investigation of that extraordinary episode led me to understand that facts of significance in relations between American Jewry and Zionists are not so much "hidden" today as omitted.

Jacob Blaustein's speech is an excellent illustration of when the omissions started, and the reasons. We see a key moment when that American Jewish world transformed to ours:

- the creation of now-familiar methods of defense and justification for the State of Israel, and

- the exclusion, from the American Jewish mainstream, of questioning political nationalism of the Jewish people.

Baltimore, the site of Blaustein's speech, was a center of both Zionist and anti-Zionist American Jewish activity. It was the home of Henrietta Szold, founder of Hadassah, the Women's Zionist Organization of America, and Rabbi Morris S. Lazaron, a founder of the anti-Zionist American Council for Judaism.

In the speech, we see the moment when the die is cast for American Jewish policy to the new State of Israel, and the arguments that will be asserted:

- that the State of Israel is an American ally; is essentially like the US in values and culture; and represents US interests in the middle east.[*]

- that US Jews should be both innocent of political connection to

---

5 See chapter "The Ben Gurion-Blaustein 'Exchange of Views'—1950," page 184.
* This has a chimerical quality depending on the needs of the time: during the Cold War, the Labor government of Israel was presented as an important ally to stem international Communist progress, and now Israel is a bulwark against "Islamic extremism."

the "foreign" State of Israel, and at the same time fraternally helpful.

- that the State of Israel only acts with force when that is necessitated by irrational adversaries, but hopes for reasoned settlement of conflicts, as the benign nature of its aims are finally recognized.

- that the creation of Arab refugees was regrettable; existence of Jewish refugees was intolerable.

More broadly, we see Blaustein, a major American Jewish leader:

- who saw combating Jewish nationalism as an important value for the welfare of Jews.

- who knew the State of Israel flag as a banner of a factional movement, Zionism, within Jewry.

- who after the state's creation faithfully advocated for the new state to the American government.

- who valued the American Jewish way of life in a heterogeneous and non-sectarian country.

- whose vision of the Jewish settlement in Palestine was of a homeland coexisting in equality with Palestinian Arabs.

In the ongoing wars that followed the birth of the State of Israel, arguments and explanations for Israeli policy were weapons deployed for the state. Public discussion of some facts about the state seemed weapons aimed at the Jews of Palestine, and would endanger — it was feared — Jews elsewhere.[6]

---
6 See chapter "Qibya, 1953," page 161.

Forty-seven years after Blaustein's speech, in a 1995 AJC statement, what was established as the bounded limit of institutional Jewish opinion was only intensified, with the addition of control of all Jerusalem as a manifest necessity:

> *Jews everywhere have a stake in preserving Jerusalem as the eternal and undivided capital of Israel. Moreover, the active involvement of the United States in the region has been a critical factor in preserving Israel's security and advancing the peace process. The continuing efforts by American Jews on behalf of ongoing U.S. support for Israel — diplomatic, strategic, economic and moral — remain a necessity....*
>
> *American Jews are plainly entitled to express their opinions and offer their advice on anything about which they are informed. Unanimity can no more be expected of them than it can of Israelis. American Jews must, however, recognize that statements critical of Israel or Israeli government policy are likely to be given disproportionate weight when uttered by Jews. They should speak, therefore, with prudent circumspection. In particular, they should give reasonable deference to positions taken by Israel through its regular democratic processes, especially on matters of security and defense.*[7]

American Jews were to speak softly misgivings of the Israeli ethnic state, and to advocate for the State of Israel within their own country.

Ambiguity and Clarity

THE 1948 speech reflects the dual nature of AJC pre-statehood actions, a dual nature which may explain why there was little hope they could have successfully fought full manifestation of Jewish nationalism:

- in 1918, qualified endorsement of the British (Balfour) Declaration that intended to show a

---

[7] "AJC on Israel-Diaspora Relations, A Policy Statement adopted by the Board of Governors, February 11, 1995," http://www.ajc.org/site/apps/nl/newsletter2.asp?c=ijITI2PHKoG&b=839817

careful distance from Jewish nationalism, and commitment to the American pluralistic way.

- in 1924, leadership in the formation of the Jewish Agency for Palestine, which was intended to have a full spectrum of leadership from the Jewish community, including the non-Zionists.

- in 1946-47, support for a Jewish-majority partitioned area within Palestine, to be Jewish only in the sense that America was "Christian," by majority within a civil nation.

In the speech, a pattern is set — violence by nationalist Jews in Palestine is excised from discussion, and the American Jewish Committee would not treat the emerging State of Israel as an alien force, even as it incarnated the "worldwide Jewish nationalism" the AJC deplored.

Public demur from the methods or worldview of Israel will be severely muted, as in the 1995 AJC recommendation that American Jews speak with "prudent circumspection" any criticism of Israeli policy.[8]

In earlier years, the AJC had experienced stinging "criticism and invective" from Zionists, when it attempted to distinguish between helping Jews in Palestine and building a national Jewish state. In 1943, "The Committee was accused of having broken unity in Jewish life, and therefore betrayed the Jewish people."[9]

Blaustein's and AJC President-emeritus Joseph Proskauer's later efforts to extract the Blaustein-Ben Gurion Statement from the Israeli executive — of respect for Jewish life outside the State of Israel — ran counter to the larger "Zionising" of diaspora life, foreseen in a late 1947 AJC memo on Zionist planning.[10]

The moment passed when the AJC could have publicly said it had been "misled" by the Zionists in the pre-Statehood period of broad cooperation to fight for open Jewish immigration to Palestine, as Blaustein imagined doing in October 1949.[11]

---

8   *Ibid.*
9   Morris D. Waldman, *Nor By Power,* International Universities Press, New York, 1953, page 265.
10 See page 127.
11 See page 180.

Jewish Violence and the Urgency for Partition

AN ARTICLE by newsman Hal Lehrman in the March 1948 *Commentary* magazine* illustrates the already well-developed and effective forces with which non-nationalist Jews were contending:

> The State Department had long foreseen that the Arabs would violently resist partition. The State Department had clearly said so. For its pains, the State Department was branded as anti-Jewish in Zionist propaganda. Its advice was outweighed by pro-partition planks in the Democratic and Republican platforms and by pro-partition resolutions in Congress. After having refused, because of Zionist insistence, to share the responsibility for plans which might have worked, the United States, again because of Zionist pressure, finally committed itself in the UN to partition—the one plan which had no hope of succeeding at all.[12]

The rationale of the partition plan was to create a peaceful solution for both major groups in Palestine. The urgent militancy which partition was intended to blunt came from within the *Yishuv* (Palestine Jewish community):

> "What we need now, an Irgun major told me, is not a boundary but enough immigrants and guns. Then we'll be ready to carve out a real Palestine—both halves of partition and Transjordan as well—by the only methods that the Arabs (and the world) respect: force."[13] [14]

---

* Although the AJC published *Commentary* magazine, it was intended to contain a wide-range of views. The *Committee Reporter* was the organ of the AJC.

12 Hal Lehrman, "Partition in Washington: An Inquiry. The Factors Guiding Our Government's Policy," *Commentary*, March 1948, page 208.

13 *Ibid*, page 211-212.

14 In 1949, a CIA analysis was that "If boundaries to an Israeli State, any boundaries, had been set and guaranteed by the Great Powers, peace might return to the area. On the contrary, we have actually a victorious state which is limited to no frontiers and which is determined that no narrow limits shall be set. The Near East is faced with the almost certain prospect of a profound and growing disturbance by Israel which may last for decades. Instead of restoring the boundaries of the province of Judea as they were in 70 AD, the Israeli leaders now state freely, though usually unofficially, their demand for an ever-expanding empire. Their present possessions are regarded by them only as a beachhead into the Arab and Muslim world, a large part of which they intend to exploit. They are not prepared to live off what the land will yield as the Arabs do." "Observations Concerning Palestine and the Arab Countries," March 18, 1949, page 2, www.foia.cia.gov.

Blaustein in his speech lays out the positive case, that on the success of partition, "American Jews, together with their government, would be on the side of the United Nations, exactly as they sided with the democratic powers during the World Wars."

Left, discarded, in the February 8 draft of the speech is the negative case — that before partition, "terrorist groups of Palestinian Jews took the offensive" and that "If Partition fails, it is more than likely that these Jewish extremists will resort to terrorism and violence in spite of efforts to control them."

Remaining in the speech, is that the advantage of partition is that in future the American press "would stress that it is the Arabs, and not the Jews, who are taking the offensive in defiance of a decision of the United Nations."

The atmosphere that Jewish terrorism created, forcing the AJC decision to support partition, is described in the draft speech text.[15]

It is reasonable to suppose that if the UN had not approved partition of Palestine, the Irgun and other "underground" Jewish groups would have expanded their extensive bombing campaign to London and Washington — and the word "Zionist" would today have the same flavor of fanaticism as "Irish Republican" or "Islamist," for Americans.

Certainly the vigor of their violence within Palestine was decisive.

Lehrman described in *Commentary*:
> *If public opinion in Britain demands an end to the disastrous occupation of Palestine, it is in no small part due to the effectiveness of Jewish terrorists with landmine, grenade, pistol, and rope against unfortunate men wearing the King's colors.*
> *"The terrorists defeated us," British officers admit. "We couldn't track them down. The Jewish population was too frightened of them to help us."*[16]

Jewish extremist violence was already spilling out of Palestine into Europe.[17]

---

15 See page 24.
16 Lehrman, *ibid*, page 212.
17 As described on this Irgun historical website: "After organization and consolidation, it was decided to commence operational activity, and the first target selected was the British Embassy in Rome....[October 31, 1946] At 2:46 am, there was a loud explosion

The removed passages in Blaustein's speech clarify that an impetus and urgency for supporting partition was the Jewish terrorist campaign, and the expectation of more. (A New York Times article about a suspected Irgun bombing of a British troop train in Austria in August 1947 said, "A report from the British zone said that it had been discovered recently that about 200 Jewish displaced persons in one center had joined the Zionist underground organization."[18])

Albert Einstein, Hannah Arendt, Sidney Hook and others wrote that in the years up to statehood, Jewish terrorists "inaugurated a reign of terror in the Palestine Jewish community. Teachers were beaten up for speaking against them, adults were shot for not letting their children join them. By gangster methods, beatings, window-smashing, and widespread robberies, the terrorists intimidated the population and exacted a heavy tribute."[19]

In December 1947 AJC analyst Milton Himmelfarb wrote there had been two reasons for the AJC change of position on partition. The first was the need for an immediate refuge for DPs.

> *The second reason is that it gradually became clear that failure to establish a Jewish state could bring about perhaps a worse state of affairs than the actual establishment of the state. The terrorists' activities in Palestine, and the posterings and mouthings of their supporters here and abroad, led a number of AJC people to wonder whether a Jewish state was the chief enemy. They began to feel that after the state was created, the daily papers in New York at least would no longer carry headlines screaming of King David Hotel explosions and hangings of British sergeants; in short, "better an evil end than an endless evil."*[20]

---

and the central section of the building was destroyed. ...Meanwhile, branches had been set up in various parts of Europe, and attempts were made to strike at British targets, such as the Sacher Hotel in Vienna, the regional British army headquarters. The explosion there caused light damage to the building, but the propaganda impact was considerable. A train transporting British troops was sabotaged, and an explosion occurred in the hotel in Vienna which housed the offices of the British occupation force." http://www.etzel.org.il/english/ac16.htm. Also see page 135.

18 "Irgun's Hand Seen in Alps Rail Blast," *New York Times*, August 16, 1947, page 4.
19 "New Palestine Party. Visit of Begin and Aims of Political Movement Discussed." Joint letter to the New York Times, December 4, 1948, page 12. Letter protests visit of Herut party leader Menachem Begin to the United States..
20 Milton Himmelfarb, "AJC Position on the Jewish State," 6-page memo, mimeo, December 31, 1947, page 5, binder "Record of the American Jewish Committee in Re

The AJC's Public Posture

THE AJC had tried to maintain a distinction between support of a haven for distressed Jews versus zealotry of the political goal of a Jewish state. In these efforts, it may have been too subtle by half. One observer is quoted in a February 1948 AJC document:

> The Agency is the captive of the terrorists; American non-Zionists are captives of the Agency. As a result, the Stern Gang and the AJC are saying the same things—at least the AJC is saying nothing different, as far as the American public or American Jewry can see.[21] [22]

That impression may not have been corrected by efforts such as this January 19, 1948 letter to the New York Herald Tribune from AJC Pres. Joseph M. Proskauer:

> The responsible Jews in Palestine are engaged in no struggle of aggression or of aggrandizement. If any hot-headed group is acting at variance with this position, that group is disavowed.[23]

The mechanism of the change of the American Jewish Committee's position — from opposition to "Jewish nationalism" to lobbyist for the new state — is illuminated in the speech.

Creation of a taboo against public opposition to Zionism is laid out for the American Jewish community. The American Jewish Committee's effort to make the Council for American Judaism "cease" public criticism

---

Palestine," Vol. 3, AJC. The volumes appear to have been assembled in 1953, and have adhesive stars applied to their spines. This author was told by AJC archive staff the star was an indication of confidential material. This passage is similar to a passage in Blaustein's draft speech; see page 25.

Himmelfarb concludes — in an exemplar of Louis Marshall's warning in 1918 that the Zionists had poetry on their side (see page 77n) — that "those of our contemporaries who fear Jewish nationalism cannot avoid being stirred by the establishment of a Third Commonwealth two thousand years after the destruction of the Second and three thousand after the founding of the First."

21 "Notes for a Non-Zionist Palestine Policy for American Jews," 2/11/48, page 10, "Record of the American Jewish Committee in RE Palestine," Vol. 4, AJC.
22 November 2, 1946, in an AJC Subcommittee on Palestine meeting, "Fear was expressed that an invitation to the AJC to see Bevin that will come through Nahum Goldmann, will be interpreted as an endorsement of the Agency plan, and makes the AJC a tail to the Agency's kite." AJC Staff Meeting folder, FAD-1, BOX 78 ("Israel"), RG347.7.1, YIVO.
23 *AJC Committee Reporter*, February 1948, vol. 5 no. 2.

of American Zionism grew from this.[24] The AJC also intended "criticism, internally and in the Jewish press, of extremist Jewish nationalist positions"[25] — to foster a Jewish American golden mean.

In the speech[26] is the "anti-Zionism aids anti-Semitism" syllogism:

> 1. Anti-Semites make use of anti-Zionist statements of Jews.
> 2. Zionists are part of the Jewish people.
> 3. Speaking against Zionism helps anti-Semites.

Often, a correlate is that support of Zionism is US policy, so that opposition to Zionism is opposition to US policy and interests.[27] [28]

A January 1948 "confidential" policy summary said that by acceding to an "inevitable" partition decision, the Committee took "the only way out of an otherwise unsolvable and untenable situation towards a new and more workable stage in the setting of which we, ourselves, today may take a strong hand." The AJC hoped its actions would leave it "the necessary moral and political standing and authority within the community to be heard and followed as a leader in the right direction, through the difficulties and pitfalls of the future."[29]

Blaustein and the AJC tried to curb Jewish nationalism and identification of Jews with the State of Israel, but within definite limits of a "propriety" that limited full debate among American Jews in public fora.[30]

---

24 See chapter "The AJC vs the ACJ," page 200.
25 "Notes for a Non-Zionist Palestine Policy for American Jews," 2/11/48, page 15.
26 See page 46, clause "h."
27 See Louis Marshall to Max Senor, page 83.
28 In 1948, AJC vice president Alan M. Stroock reported to the committee Jan. 16-18 annual meeting, in an example of the endless "geopolitical" calculations of American interests to which discussions of Israel can descend, that "Russia is interested in the very sections in which the Jewish state exists. Other powers are also interested in that section. We cannot ignore the fact that a large minority in Palestine has expressed views friendly to Russia, and if the arms embargo continues, those leanings will become more pronounced and prominent." Allen M. Stroock, "The Palestine Situation Today," AJC 41st Annual Report, page 133.
29 "Political Problems involved in the Palestine Solution," January 13, 1948, page 1, in binder "Record of the American Jewish Committee in RE Palestine," Vol. 4, AJC. See the AJC's determination to retain influence, and avoid the pariah status of the anti-Zionist American Council for Judaism, pages 98 and 181.
30 The AJC rebuked the (anti-Zionist) American Council for Judaism, not because of disagreement with their opinions, but that they publicized them before gentiles. In

By 1953, rather than leading the situation, the AJC was working to protect diaspora Jews from the consequences of a "Jewish state," as became clear in the aftermath of the Qibya Massacre[31] — proving out Moshe Sharett's statement that Jews "throughout the world" would be hostage to Zionist conduct in Palestine.[32]

1948 — THE STATE OF ISRAEL IS DECLARED

THE YEAR of the speech is the year when AJC began its support for the State of Israel with the United States executive and legislative branches. The contrast can be seen with 1944, when AJC Pres. Proskauer wrote Undersecretary of State Edward R. Stettinius, Jr. that the AJC rejected "the nationalist theory of Jewish life."[33]

The year 1948 is when the name Israel changed – no more the Jewish people of the world, but a particular State holding particular territory, with the powers and vices of a State.

The change is a dramatic and conflicted one. In 1949-50, Proskauer and Blaustein attempted to tame Jewish nationalism — explicitly to contest the claim of Israel to be the Jewish State. What in 2009 Prime Minister Netanyahu demanded of the Palestinian Authority[34] — recognition of Israel as "the nation state of the Jewish people" — Blaustein insisted Ben Gurion deny in the Ben Gurion-Blaustein "Agreement" or "Exchange" or "Statement" of 1950.[35]

1950, Blaustein wrote Lessing Rosenwald that they shared a "mutual abhorrence for world Jewish political nationalism." See page 203.
31 See page 161.
32 See page 168.
33 See page 113.
34 Benjamin Netanyahu, Prime Minister of the State of Israel, speech at Bar-Ilan University, June 14 2009, http://www.mfa.gov.il/MFA/Government/Speeches+by+Israeli+leaders/2009/Address_PM_Netanyahu_Bar-Ilan_University_14-Jun-2009.htm "Therefore, a fundamental prerequisite for ending the conflict is a public, binding and unequivocal Palestinian recognition of Israel as the nation state of the Jewish people. ...any demand for resettling Palestinian refugees within Israel undermines Israel's continued existence as the state of the Jewish people."
35 In 1918, Lionel de Rothschild of the League of British Jews did get commitments from the Zionist Organization — that they would not claim there is a worldwide Jewish

The draft of Blaustein's speech is remarkable for the clarity about what AJC support for partition did not mean — "We do this, however, not for political reasons or a desire to establish a so-called Jewish state."[36] The biggest achievement of Zionists in the United States since 1948 has been establishing a Jewish state as definitive of Jewish identity.

In the speech, Blaustein listed elements that muted opposition to political Zionism in the American Jewish community:

1. The trauma of the Holocaust, exceeding in horror even the persecutions of Eastern Europe a generation before.

2. The existence of hundreds of thousands of Jewish Displaced Persons (DPs) in camps, almost three years after the end of the European war.

There was, however, contention over how many DPs would actually choose Palestine if America or other countries were open.[37] Alfred M. Lilienthal of the anti-Zionist American Council for Judaism (ACJ) wrote, "...Europe's Displaced Persons had to be powerfully 'convinced' that Israel was the only place where they could build their lives anew."[38]

By May 1948, Rabbi Abraham J. Klausner, who had worked with Jewish DPs since arriving at Dachau in May 1945, wrote to the American Jewish Conference that Jewish aid groups should determine that "these people must go to Palestine... They are not to be asked, but to be told, what to do. They will be thankful in years to come."[39]

In a poignant twist, Nahum Goldmann of the Jewish Agency commented that that the DPs were not particularly desirable *olim*

---

nationality, and would not attempt to set up a state eventually in Palestine that privileged Jews over non-Jews — in exchange for a League endorsement of the Balfour Declaration. See page 80.

36 Page 25.
37 The Zionist strategy in the creation and direction of the numbers of DPs in camps is illuminated in "Holocaust Survivors as a Political Factor", Zeev Tzahor, *Middle Eastern Studies*, Vol. 24, No. 4 (Oct., 1988), pp. 432-444.) The Jewish Agency maximized in every way possible the prominence of Palestine as the sole goal of DPs. See also Irgun compulsion in the DP camps in *Taking Sides*, Stephen Green, William Morrow and Co., New York, 1984, page 48-51.
38 Alfred M. Lilienthal, *What Price Israel,* Regnery Publishing, 1953, page 148.
39 Page 149, *ibid.* Also in Rabbi Klausner's 2002 book, *A letter to my children from the edge of the Holocaust*

(immigrants) for Israel, and had outlived their propaganda usefulness as an argument for the United Nations partition vote the previous November.[40]

Blaustein and the AJC were conscious of the presence and importance of the Arab population of Palestine, and reluctantly favored Partition beginning in 1946 to allow a Jewish-majority area, but with a distinctly American goal for that area of a mixed Jewish and Arab state.[41]

The post-Israeli statehood activities of the AJC was composed of three tracks:

1. Advocacy for the new State of Israel with the American government for funds, diplomatic cover for it in the international community, and arms.[42]

2. Restraining the "Jewish Nationalist" ideology of the new State, especially that implying emigration of Jews from America.

3. Marginalizing and muffling of anti-Zionist opposition to the new State, most notably of the Council for American Judaism.

In the summer of 1948, officers of the AJC closely consulted with the Provisional Government of Israel and US political figures on the emerging issues of truces, armistice lines, and Arab refugees from areas conquered by the new state.

---

40 "Minutes of Jewish Cooperating Organizations' meeting on DP situation, May 4, 1948," ajcarchives.org. "The DPs, in general, do not represent the human material Eretz Yisroel needs today. In Cyprus, in Eastern Europe, and notably in the Moslem countries we have an infinitely more desireable material available. In the interests of the State, we have to choose the better material, young, willing people, not those who have to be forced. Besides, the DPs represent no political argument for Palestine any more either. This angle does not make any impression on General [Secretary of State] Marshall any more, it is therefore a politically irrelevant thing from the point of view of the Jewish State. We have reached the brutal phase where the interests of the State count alone."

41 See Rabbi Philipson's testimony to the US Congress in 1922 that Zionism brought "the east European attitude to America...the state of mind that the Jews are a separate group, a separate national group," page 66.

42 "Israeli and Zionist leaders perceived the AJC as the Jewish organization with the best access to U.S. policy-makers and as most representative of wealthy American Jews. Thus, the AJC was an important link in securing political and economic support from the American government and financial assistance from the American Jewish community." Charles S. Liebman, "Diaspora Influence on Israel: The Ben-Gurion-Blaustein 'Exchange' and its Aftermath," *Jewish Social Studies*, Vol. XXXVI, Nos. 3-4 (July-October 1974), page 271-272.

Initiation of a pattern of pressure and reward for American public officials by partisans for the new state is illustrated in discussions during Blaustein's involvement in financing the 1948 Democratic presidential re-election campaign.[43]

The Mission of the AJC — Understanding its Support for Israel

The AJC articles of incorporation can explain AJC support for the new State of Israel. Despite not favoring a national Jewish state, the AJC was pledged to protect rights and welfare of Jews "in any part of the world."[44]

When the State of Israel was declared in 1948, and the territories of the new nation expanded in war past the portion allotted to it in the partition plan — with a vast emptying of Arabs as refugees — the AJC continued succor and advocacy for Jews in Palestine. For the AJC it was a continuation of their work for coreligionists abroad, but the meaning of their actions qualitatively changed.

In April 1950, a high-level AJC "Committee on the Impact of Israel" re-examined the policy of support for the Jewish settlement in Palestine that strengthened the State of Israel in its conflicts: "American dollars (from Jews) sent and spent in good faith for relief in Israel can nevertheless be said to further the military program of a foreign state."[45]

---

43 See chapter "Advocacy for the New State," page 149.
44 "The objects of this corporation shall be, to prevent the infraction of the civil and religious rights of Jews, in any part of the world; to render all lawful assistance and to take appropriate remedial action in the event of threatened or actual invasion or restriction of such rights, or of unfavorable discrimination with respect thereto; to secure for Jews equality of economic, social and educational opportunity; to alleviate the consequences of persecution and to afford relief from calamities affecting Jews, wherever they may occur; and to compass these ends to administer any relief fund which shall come into its possession or which may be received by it, in trust or otherwise, for any of the aforesaid objects or for purposes comprehended therein." AJC Articles of Incorporation, AJYB, Vol. 13 (1911-12).
45 See page 162. The hazard of American Jews becoming enmeshed with a nascent foreign country with different principles and goals was anticipated by speakers in a 1924 conference on Palestine chaired AJC President Louis Marshall (see page 74), and the spectre of "dual allegiance" was always a concern, and is denied as a possibility twice in Blaustein's speech.

It became apparent that the impact on the status of Jews in the diaspora (the Jewish world outside of Palestine) by the actions of the new state could not be ignored, and in the crisis year of 1953 (Jordan River diversion at B'not Yaakov; Qibya Massacre of civilians by Israeli commandos) the AJC determined that its mission of protecting the safety and welfare of Jews meant that it had to do more "public relations" work advocating for Israeli policy.[46] It turned to the Israeli government for material — information and arguments — for that work.[47]

The American Jewish Committee was not new to the process. In 1948, on the imminent declaration of the State of Israel, it determined — while avoiding material "too strongly propagandistic" from Zionist organizations — to prepare a
> *fact sheet for columnists, editors and other public media personnel in preparing information of "making the desert bloom" type... [and promote the idea of] a friendly Jewish Palestine as a defense against Communism.*[48]

The way Jacob Blaustein interpreted the mission of the American Jewish Committee, and forbore to publicly express and thus legitimize Jewish opposition to the more aggressive implications of Zionist ideology, is a story setting Palestine's fate. His opposition to the Jewish nationalist philosophy coexisted, functionally, with support of every kind that a Jewish American citizen could provide to the State of Israel.

In Jacob Blaustein's advocacy for the new state there is a "twinning" with Israeli actions confounding each intention:

- with his assertion there is no "dual loyalty" danger in American Jews' identification with the new state,
    - the repetition from the state's leaders that Jews belong in Israel.[49]

- with the AJC's construction of the American image of Israel as an America-like pioneering and open society built on values shared with the United States,
    - the privileging of one ethnic group in antithesis to the American ideal, reflected in a 1952 Knesset bill establishing

---
46 See page 166.
47 See page 167.
48 See page 128.
49 See efforts to restrain Jewish nationalism, and the Ben Gurion-Blaustein exchange, pages 178 and 184.

that "The State of Israel regards itself as the creation of the entire Jewish people" and tasking the Jewish Agency with expanding to represent Jews world-wide.[50]
- with Jacob's belief that a "heart to heart talk" with both sides by a trusted mediator could lead to neighborly Israeli-Arab relations,
  - hostile actions by Israel to Palestinians Arabs and neighboring states.[51]

Three surprising facts emerge from the study of Jacob Blaustein's relation to the invention of the State of Israel:

1. His lack of enthusiasm — disdain — for Zionist casting of Jews as eternal "outsiders" in the world, the central tenet of the logic of taking Palestine for Jews.

2. His extraordinary centrality and effectiveness influencing the United States in the key early years of Israeli statehood.

3. His leadership in creating a practice of American Jewish "non-opposition" among "non-Zionists" to the new Zionist reality.

---

50 http://www.israellawresourcecenter.org/israellaws/fulltext/jewishagencystatuslaw.htm The bill declared, "The mission of gathering in the exiles, which is the central task of the State of Israel and the Zionist Movement in our days, requires constant efforts by the Jewish people in the Diaspora; the State of Israel, therefore, expects the cooperation of all Jews, as individuals and groups, in building up the State and assisting the immigration to it of the masses of the people, and regards the unity of all sections of Jewry as necessary for this purpose." This is titled "World Zionist Organization - Jewish Agency (Status) Law."
51 See Arab refugees, Qibya raid of 1953, Operation Susannah of 1954, and Gaza raid of 1955, pages 193, 161 and 171.

Jacob Blaustein to the Baltimore Chapter, American Jewish Committee, February 15, 1948

'THE MEANING OF PALESTINE PARTITION FOR AMERICAN JEWS'

Prepared
from

The Collected Personal and Business Papers of Louis and Jacob Blaustein, MS 400, Special Collections, Milton S. Eisenhower Library, The Johns Hopkins University, Baltimore, Maryland.

Text of draft speech, deleted from final address, is in **bold** type on gray background.

News clipping from box 3.31, folder "1947 Palestine Clippings," JHU.

February 15, 1948

'THE MEANING OF PALESTINE PARTITION FOR AMERICAN JEWS'

INTRODUCTION

1 - It in always good to report to you, here at home. We know each other. We know that while we may at times have differences of opinion on questions affecting Jewry, we nevertheless can have, and do have, faith in each other's integrity and respect for each other's point of view.

2 - Addressing you members and friends of the Baltimore Chapter of the American Jewish Committee is a privilege I have exercised only on special occasions. This is considered such an occasion, for no question in Jewish life has given us, and is today giving us, more concern than that from which stems our subject tonight:

> **A - none of us want a monopoly (for, of) being called right - that's (unimportant, not important). Each of us wants to do and contribute whatever he can towards (a, the) solution of an age-old (question) problem, (and) toward making the world a better place in which to live.**
>
> **2 - (Addressing, talking to) you members and friends of the Baltimore Chapter of the American Jewish Committee is a privilege I have exercised only on special occasions.**
>
> **A - As I recall (those occasions, them), they were:**
>
> **a - In   of   , (when, at the time) the Baltimore Chapter was organized;**
>
> **b - In June (?) of 1945, when I returned from the San Francisco United Nations Conference (as a Consultant to the American**

*Jacob Blaustein's Speech, February 15, 1948. Text that was discarded is in **bold** type on gray background.*

**Delegation (there);
  c - (Again, in May of 1946, when I (got back, returned) from (serving as head of the American Delegation to) the memorable London Conference of Jewish Organizations;
  d - (And again and lastly, in October of 1946, (upon my return, when I returned from (serving as the head of the American Jewish Committee delegation to) the Paris Peace Conference and the (Conference, meeting) in Frankfort with General Joseph T. McNarney (United States Commander, at the time, of the European Theater) and his Chiefs of Staff (in Frankfort), and (from) the survey (made) at his (invitation, suggestion) of the Jewish Displaced Persons Camps in Germany.
A - Mr. Oppenheimer, Rabbi Lieberman and (our, your) other local officials (have informed me (- and I believe rightly so -) (that they) consider this another such required occasion, for it seems (correct, fair) to say that no (Jewish no question (in (American) in Jewish life, (affecting (Jewry) has given us, and is today giving us, (as much, more concern (, if as much,) than that from which stems (my, our) subject tonight:**

'THE MEANING OF PALESTINE PARTITION FOR AMERICAN JEWS'

3 - This is a difficult assignment, - particularly at a moment like this when so many international factors are involved and when the day-to-day turn of events are so frequent, striking and unpredictable. I am no prophet and sometimes events have a way of running ahead of, or contrary to, even the best-reasoned

Jacob Blaustein's Speech, February 15, 1948.
Text that was discarded is in **bold** type on gray background.

expectations and judgment.
4 - I can say, though, that we have applied ourselves constantly and assiduously to the problem of Palestine. We have not dealt with it superficially. And the thinking is not only that of the few of us known to you, but includes that of scholars, scientists and other persons of experience on the scene and behind the scene.

We have also had the opportunity of conferring on the problem on more than one occasion with Presidents Roosevelt and Truman; with our various Secretaries of State and other high officials of this and other governments; and with anti-Zionists, non-Zionists and Zionists, including members of the Jewish Agency both in this country and abroad.

5 - We think we know the questions with respect to Partition that honestly and sincerely beset you - because in arriving at our decisions, the same questions undoubtedly occurred to us. I shall try to deal with several of the most important of them, and then indicate what, in my opinion, the course of conduct of the American Jew should be.

8 - This evening, I shall depart from my usual practice of talking without reference to notes, or text. Instead, because of the gravity of the (subject, situation) - and so I will not be misunderstood or misquoted - I shall confine myself (quite) (closely, largely) to my text.

I - AMERICAN JEWISH COMMITTEE HAS NOT CHANGED ITS FUNDAMENTAL POSITION

1. - As this is an American Jewish Committee sponsored meeting, I shall first answer one question some people are asking; 'Did the American Jewish Committee change its fundamental position when it went along with Partition?'

   A - The answer is `No` - the American Jewish Committee has not changed its fundamental position. The Committee played a role in the reaching of the final momentous decision to partition Palestine, but its policy has been consistent throughout.

B - In this connection, we might recall what Ralph Waldo Emerson once remarked, that 'a foolish consistency is the hobgoblin of little minds'. That remark is just, - if consistency is adhered to for its own sake, without regard to the realities of a situation. But on the one at hand, the American Jewish Committee does not have to take refuge behind a quotation. From the very beginning, our stand on Palestine was rooted in reality, and we have had no occasion to change its fundamentals since. Let me give you the sequence of events.

C - We hailed the Balfour Declaration in 1918 for what it was - a chance for Jews who aspired to live in Palestine to do so, and more particularly a chance for the persecuted Jews of the world to have Palestine as a place and a home where they could live in peace and dignity. We wanted the doors of Palestine to be open to unrestricted immigration of all Jews who wished to go there to the actual limits of its absorptive capacity. We wanted Palestine to become in due course, a self-governing, independent and democratic commonwealth, with proper safeguards for the religious, political and civil rights of <u>all</u> its inhabitants.

We made it plain that American Jews would continue to give their whole allegiance to <u>this</u> country, and to no other; and that the same thing would apply to Jews residing in other countries, with respect to their countries. From that position we have never receded.

D - When Hitlerism swept Germany and, later, most of Europe, we redoubled our efforts to aid the hapless victim of persecution to escape. Palestine was <u>one</u> important place of refuge for Jews; and that was why we denounced the British White Paper of 1939, the purpose of which was to bar the gates to all but a thin trickle of immigration and to put practically an end to the purchase of land on which they might live and flourish.

But we did not consider then, nor do we <u>now</u>, that Palestine is the <u>only</u> place to which these

Jacob Blaustein's Speech, February 15, 1948.
Text that was discarded is in **bold** type on gray background.

unfortunates should go; nor did we consider - as the extreme, political Zionists insisted in the Biltmore Declaration - that the solution lie in an immediate Jewish state of the whole of Palestine. That would have meant a minority of 600,000 Jews ruling a majority of 1,200,000 Arabs. That would have been undemocratic and, in addition, in our opinion, was unrealistic.

E - The `Statement of Views` of the American Jewish Committee, promulgated at the beginning of 1943, reiterated our considered position. The same stand was taken in our testimony before the Anglo-American Committee of Inquiry. First things must come first; and those first things meant the saving of Jewish lives; not argumentative discussions over the ultimate political constitution of Palestine.

F - But the British in 1945 turned down the recommendations of the Anglo-American Committee of inquiry which it itself had set up, and made it clear that it would insist on a solution of the political problem before it would consent to any relaxation of its immigration and land purchase policies.

G - At this time, certain members of the Jewish Agency proposed a plan for the Partition of Palestine into two sections, in one of which there would be an already existing Jewish majority of population and in the other an already existing Arab majority, both sections to enjoy full autonomy, including control of immigration, and an adequate guarantee of full democratic rights to all inhabitants, Jews, Arabs and Christians. Economic experts who studied the proposed probable Jewish area agree that it could in due time become a viable self-supporting state.

H - In view of the intransigent stand of the British in insisting on a political solution first, our Committee decided that the solution proposed by these members of the Jewish Agency, though far from ideal, would in no way contravene the democratic principles for which the American Jewish Committee has always stood. For bear in mind that the Jewish section, when thought of in terms of a

Jewish state, will be a Jewish state only in the sense that the United States, with a preponderance of Christian population, might be termed a Christian state.

Accordingly, our Executive Committee agreed that since there was no other solution then apparent which would assure a haven in Palestine for the displaced Jews of Europe and since so many human lives were at stake, an early practical compromise was preferable to any continued search for ideal solutions.

I - On April 2, 1947 the British government placed the problem in the hands of the United Nations Assembly. Two months later Judge Proskauer and I, acting under authority of our Executive Committee, presented a brief to the United Nations Special Committee on Palestine, known us UNSCOP, which, among other things, recommended: a United Nations trusteeship; an immediate grant of 100,000 immigration certificates during 1947 and subsequent maximum immigration; and steps toward ultimate complete self- government with full equality for all citizens. These were <u>first</u> things.

But <u>if</u> an immediate political solution was considered preferable by the U. N. Assembly, <u>then</u> we suggested that Palestine be partitioned along the lines advocated by those members of the Jewish Agency.

While UNSCOP was studying the situation, tension in Palestine mounted to a new high. Terrorism and counter-terrorism, reprisals and counter-reprisals were the order of the day. We condemned both the terroristic acts perpetrated by small extremist groups, as well as the British provocation and retaliation; and pointed out that these deplorable incidents emphasized the absolute necessity for competent action by the United Nations.

J - I will not burden you with the details of the final

Jacob Blaustein's Speech, February 15, 1948.
Text that was discarded is in **bold** type on gray background.

majority and minority reports by the UNSCOP committee, nor their unanimous recommendations, excepting to state that the majority proposed a scheme of Partition.

As previously stated, the American Jewish Committee had felt that an international trusteeship for a number of years would be preferable to immediate or early independence; but there was no way left other than the latter after UNSCOP came out with the majority and minority reports. Only two alternatives retained real significance - Partition or Arab domination. The choice for a responsible Jewish organization was limited. It is easy for some to sit on the sidelines and say the solution should have been something different. But nothing different was then practical or possible.

But what would have been the alternatives? The Jewish D Ps left [in] camps with the (very likely) consequences of an (anticipated) uprising (in the face of a continuing Palestinian impasse) (and violence in Palestine)

(In the meantime) it (gradually) became clear that failure to establish Partition could bring about perhaps a worse state of affairs (as far as American Jews were concerned ?) than the (actual) establishment of a state.) The terrorist activities and vicious propaganda of their supporters here and abroad, lead many who had opposed a (Jewish ?) state to wonder if it would be the chief danger.)

So we supported the views of the American government in 1946 favoring partition and we are suporting the views of the U.N. minority [sic] report for Partition now. We do this, however, not for political reasons or a desire to

Jacob Blaustein's Speech, February 15, 1948.
Text that was discarded is in **bold** type on gray background.

establish a so-called Jewish state. As stated above, there was no (worthwhile) alternative. According to UNSCOP (and the U N Assembly) it was either Partition or Arab domination (and consequent Jewish violence). We (reluctantly) chose Partition.

So we supported the views of the American government in 1946 favoring Partition. The plan of Partition as finally developed was passed in the United Nations General Assembly on November 29, 1947 by a vote of 33 to 13. We are supporting it.

K - (October 1, 1948 is the deadline for the two states to become fully independent.) Meanwhile, the British have announced the likelihood that they will withdraw their troops prior to the August 1, 1948 date for same, and there are heavy forebodings as to what will happen in the interval.

a - Even now, as you know, with British troops still on hand, acts of violence initiated by the Arabs are taking a (shocking) toll of human lives. We have appealed to the United Nations to take early steps to enforce its solemn decision and safeguard those lives.

L - The work of the American Jewish Committee, of course, is not finished with respect to Palestine. There is much more we must do positively and prevent negatively. I shall refer to these items later.

K - I want to reiterate that our policy has been thoroughly consistent throughout. It has been based on one overmastering idea - to save as quickly as possible our desperate brothers overseas, to succor the displaced and the homeless - and to bring to Palestine those who want to go there, so they can

Jacob Blaustein's Speech, February 15, 1948.
Text that was discarded is in **bold** type on gray background.

once more take root, breathe the vital air of freedom and regain their precious heritage as Jews and human beings. A political solution has not been our specific goal. And since Partition docs not contradict the democratic principles for which we have always stood, we have accepted it as the best available means to an end.

II - <u>NOW AS TO THE QUESTION SOME ARE ASKING: `HOW WILL THE POSITION OF THE JEW IN AMERICA BE AFFECTED BY PARTITION?'</u>

1 - There are some who may feel that the position of the American Jew will be adversely affected. I do not believe that these people are thinking selfishly, but are thinking rather in terms of continuing American Jewry as a strong community.

A - We Jews know the difference between a right and a wrong. And we know that it would not be right for us to live here in peace and comfort and not do what we can to alleviate the condition of our distressed brethren overseas. We realize that means not only relief for the necessities of life, but the opportunity to live again in peace and dignity.

We in America, have become the custodian of an age-old tradition. It devolves on us to remain true to the great lineage which began with the Hebrew prophets and still lives on in acts of selfless devotion and compassion for our fellow-beings.

If the people who raise this question of possible adverse effect on the Jew in America had had the experience I had - an experience I shall never forget - on the survey of DP camps in Germany, they, too, would realize (in spite of their misgivings) the absolute necessity, from a humanitarian standpoint, of doing everything possible -- without stickling unduly about ideologies -- to have the gates of Palestine and other countries opened and widened at the earliest possible moment.

When you go to these camps and hear the heartbreaking particulars; and the displaced Jews by the hundreds follow you, crowd around you and talk with you, eagerly searching for some word of improvement of their condition, some word of hope as to when they could be moved to a country of permanent residence, you just know something fast has got to be done. There is a limit to human endurance!

> **And this need for permanent countries of residence applies not only to the persons in the DP Camps but also to (Displaced Jews in some other countries and to) Jews still residing in their European countries of origin who find it necessary to live there.)**

2 - Besides, history has shown that Jews, like other groups in any one country, cannot think of, and live for, themselves alone even if they so wish. We can no more be isolationists than individual nations can be. We just cannot shut ourselves off from situations pertaining to Jews elsewhere.

> **- including the D P situations and that of Palestine no matter how hard we might try.**
>
> **Hitler preferred that. (Before his advent there was no organized anti-semitism in this country.) But these things know no boundaries. The world is small. All liabilities are one and indivisible, - and what takes place in any part of the world is bound to have its effect and almost immediately (in every other part of the world) (on everyone of us here)).**
>
> **(b - And what we have to keep in mind is that there are other considerations in the world situation which tie into Palestine - but quite apart from Partition (as such, itself) - which might (very adversely) affect the position of the Jew in this country if there is no prompt solution of the Palestine problem.**

Jacob Blaustein's Speech, February 15, 1948.
Text that was discarded is in **bold** type on gray background.

(These (situations) are not clear cut questions of (all, what are) good and (all, what are) bad. That's the difficulty.) (I shall refer to some of these (kind of) items in another connection a little later). (NOTE: Maybe give few instances here.)
2 - The point is that there just (had, has) to be a solution. **(I know that individuals and groups, like nations, continue to hope that they can escape responsibility by delaying, holding back from action, by thinking things over just once more. I remind you, however, that they cannot. They can escape from the results of making a decision, but they cannot escape from the results of not making a decision. And these results can be equally positive, equally inexorable (?), equally lasting (good or bad))**
(A - As previously stated, there was no (suitable, acceptable) alternative after the U N made its decision: and there is none now. There is not much use talking about (fresh new,) more conferences - excepting of course, conferences for implementation under the accepted (fact, pattern) of Partition. You can't go back and start all over again. That is all Palestine has had for years - conferences and more conferences, investigating committees and more investigating committees, with nothing accomplished and increasing deterioration.)
(a - Bear in mind that if Partition were now cast aside that would not result in abrogation of the White Paper. The British and the Arabs would not have that any more now

> than when (we tried) (it, to accomplish it). So what do we have? Still violence, but with Jews bearing the world and the American stigma of instigation, instead of the Arabs being branded the offenders as now. It seems quite clear - and I do not know that we American Jews have the right and certainly would not have the power - to stop these Jews of Palestine who apparently are resolved to defend their rights to the last man, for they know that their back is (against, to) the wall and that this is the last stand.

3 - <u>A decision has been made - a decision of the majority of the world through the United Nations.</u>

    A - And what it resolves itself into, in my opinion, is this: Shall we American Jews do what we can constructively to implement that decision, with our best facilities of mind and heart? Or shall we let that implementation go by default, because we cannot summon up enough courage and wisdom to chart a course that will give the maximum benefit with the least possible penalty?

    B - There comes a time when practical people realize that endless debate on what should have been, should cease. We gain nothing by still trying to figure out, or argue, whether the United Nations should have decided on Partition. The decision was made after many months of careful investigation, hearing of evidence and deliberate consideration. Continuing argument only gives courage to the Arab aggressors who threaten the peace.

> (C - The United Nations Assembly made that decision in the face of identical threats which are now being made by the Arabs against the implementation of that decision. The United States - also in the face of these very threats - took leadership in arriving at that decision. (Both on

Jacob Blaustein's Speech, February 15, 1948.
Text that was discarded is in **bold** type on gray background.

> **and off the record the Arabs served notice on the world and on the United States that they intended by force to flout this decision (of the Assembly).**

C - As Americans and as Jews, it is our clear duty to do everything we can to have the decision implemented and, if need be, enforced; for this is not just a Jewish question, - the peace of the world, the prestige and authority of the United States and the prestige and preservation of the United Nations are involved.

(D - I might add here that as far as I know, every national Jewish organization in this country that has expressed itself, be it Zionist, non-Zionist or anti-Zionist, excepting one, is supporting Partition and asking for the implementation of it.)

4 - <u>Now some are asking whether the security of the United States does not require that Partition be dropped?</u> They talk about oil; they talk about the possibility of Russians getting into the area.

A - Of course, there are uncertainties, but I believe that any such misgivings as to what might occur <u>as a consequence of</u> Partition are greatly overstated.

B - As to Mid-East oil, it is my opinion that the Arab countries need the United States interests as much as the United States needs the Arabs' oil. While the Arabs have the oil underground, the Americana have the technique, equipment, world transportation facilities, markets and dollars. Both are important, as other countries with oil reserves have learned.

Only a few days ago, the president of the Trans-Arabian Pipe Line Company, which is owned by United States companies and is constructing the pipe line across Saudi-Arabia, Trans-Jordan, Syria and Lebanon, made public a report in which (1) he said the work is speeding up and (2) he reminded of the public assurances given by King Ibn Saud of Saudi-Arabia that activities of United States oil companies within his kingdom will be protected, regardless of what happens elsewhere.

I do not mean that threats to discontinue

Jacob Blaustein's Speech, February 15, 1948.
*Text that was discarded is in **bold** type on gray background.*

concessions may not still be made, and perhaps short cessations of work ordered, as attempted indications of Arab solidarity. But Arab solidarity does not actually exist; oil is Saudi-Arabia's only resource; and the Arabs have much to gain from the friendship of the United States in terms of material development, economic well-being. and political security.

It is not likely that these Arab countries because of the United States stand for Partition would favor, let us say Russia, with this oil, instead of the United States. Russia also voted for Partition and besides, the Arab rulers would hardly want the Russians in their midst in contact with their masses.

Yes, Russia might try to bring pressure on the Arab countries for their oil, but if Russia wishes to go that far, it can find other pretexts than that arising out of Partition. In fact, Russia might more readily do so if violence and chaos result because of Partition breaking down, on the claim of having to preserve order in the Mediterranean area, and especially if troops of a. U. N. international force are not on the scene in Palestine.

(Also, it should be borne in mind that there are considerable oil reserves in the Western Hemisphere even though our United States supply at the present time is hard pressed due to war-time drain and to meet extraordinary peace demands. By the way, our nation's oil discoveries in 1947 were the largest since 1937 and with steel and other resources made available, many additional discoveries will be made. There are also the possibilities here of synthetic petroleum products from coal, gas and oil shales.)

5- <u>Further, the security of the United States depends not alone on oil but basically and fundamentally on the preservation of the U. N.</u>

A - Partition is a test as to whether the U. N. can stand. In the United Nations may lie the future of mankind. U. N. must not go the way of the League of Nations, for with atomic weapons this may be the world's last chance.

If the United States had joined the

Jacob Blaustein's Speech, February 15, 1948.
Text that was discarded is in **bold** type on gray background.

League of Nations - and the League of Nations had been effective, we in all likelihood would not have had the Japanese invasion (in 1931) of China (Manchuko), nor Italy invade Ethiopia, nor the German invasion. And most likely there would not have been World War II.

B · It is unthinkable that the United States and the United Nations should ever take the position that the difficulties known at the time of the Assembly vote - identical threats were made by the Arabs then as now - can be made to appear so great at this time as to cause these nations to stand idly by in the Security Council and permit inaction. That would confess to the world that the very threats of violence and opposition proceeding from the Arabs - most of the Arab countries being members of the U. N., mind you - and the very unwillingness to cooperate expressed by the mandatory power, are now sufficient warrant for an admission of bankruptcy by the United Nations and a confession to the world that the United Nations is not an effective instrument of peace but a mere expression of pious hope.

(It is equally unthinkable that those whose lives are being sacrificed because of that decree should be denied the arms and means with which to defend both themselves and the action of the United Nations.)

To those who may urge the old familiar claim that brave and high principal-conduct should give way to appeasement - in this instance appeasement of the Grand Mufti who sided with the Nazis and sabotaged our war effort by every means within his power, we reply: Would such appeasement lead to peace in the troubled near East and to a solution of our problems? (Would the Arab leaders be satisfied even with a complete reversal of the United Nations action, without demanding in addition that the internationally recognized bases established by the Balfour Declaration and the League of Nations

Mandate be scrapped and that Jewish immigration be to all effect stopped and the Jews in Palestine reduced to a defenseless minority?) Would anything be gained by appeasement that would warrant our so affecting the preservation of the United Nations as to strike it a blow from which it might never recover? The very reverse is the case!

(There can be no peace in the near east unless the plan for Partition is put into effect. That was the real as well as the avowed reason for its adoption.) Even if we were to grant that the machinations of the Mufti have aggravated the difficulties anticipated at the time of the Assembly decision, shall we be blinded as to the larger principles of the security issue involved?)

Our military security depends in a very large part, and we have so recognized and stated in the past, upon the effective working of the United Nations and the implementation of its decisions.

Once that organization stands self-confessed as too weak to oppose a contemptuous disregard of its solemn mandate, then it confesses itself as a failure and a broken reed, and we proceed at once to an anarchy and chaos that holds incalculable consequences for the future of the world.

Whenever right gives way to threats - when principle is sacrificed - immediate benefits are short-lived and worse consequences later result. Thus, if Britain had not sought to appease the Arabs by the 1939 White Paper, and immigration into Palestine had not been impeded to a thin trickle and land purchases virtually stopped, there would in all probability not be this difficult Palestine situation today, not only for the Jews and Arabs but also for

Jacob Blaustein's Speech, February 15, 1948.
Text that was discarded is in **bold** type on gray background.

the world and Britain itself. Another appeasement could only result in a still more aggravated situation and catastrophe to the U. N.

   The United States urged Partition as the most effective means to promote peace in the middle East and, consequently, enhance the military security of the United States. Our military security depends in a very large part, and we have so recognized and stated in the past, upon the effective working of the United Nations and the implementation of its decisions. The support of the United Nations has been, and must continue to be, a fundamental tenet of American Foreign policy.

6 - Now that we have discussed the United States and the United Nations phases, let us turn again to more of the Jewish aspects.

   A - The anti-Semite may say the Partition of Palestine presents a problem of possible inconsistency between our obligations as Americans and as Jews in what is termed dual allegiance. This possibility also seems to be the fear[,] unfounded in my opinion, of a small segment of American Jewry.

   There is no such problem. When the American Jewish Committee endorsed the Balfour Declaration in April 1918, it expressed itself firmly on this question as follows:

> 'The Committee regards it as axiomatic that the Jews of the United States have here established a permanent home for themselves and their children, have acquired the rights and assumed the correlative duties of American citizenship, and recognize their unqualified allegiance to the United States, which they love and cherish and of whose people they constitute an integral part.'

Again in our Statement of Views of 1943 we stated, 'There can be no political identification of Jews outside of Palestine with whatever government may there be instituted.'

This continues to be the case today. It is axiomatic. Factually, there can be no real confusion about it.

Jacob Blaustein's Speech, February 15, 1948.
Text that was discarded is in **bold** *type on gray background.*

Jews of America are not split personalities politically and we shall continue to demonstrate in faith and in conduct, what we have manifested time and again on the battlefield for America, that we are an integral part and parcel of America.

Allegiance is primarily a political concept. And allegiance to the United States does not require that we cease to be interested in Palestine. Palestine remains, among other things, a Holy Land, a center for Judaism for the stimulation of our faith, for the pursuit of development of our literature, science and art in a Jewish environment.

The new Palestinian state with a preponderance of Jewish population will be a nation, as clearly, let us say, as Ireland is a nation, and Americans of Jewish faith will no more be citizens of the state in Palestine than Americans of Irish ancestry are citizens of Ireland.

I shall have a little more to say later on the question of dual allegiances.

7 - <u>Now what other doubts have been expressed as to the effect of Partition on American Jewry?</u>

A - <u>For instance, will Partition have a tendency to increase anti-Semitism in this country?</u>

One can never tell positively. Other factors, such as possible economic upheaval or disturbed social conditions, seem to me a more likely incentive. Anti-Semitism is a strange phenomena as evidenced by what Hitler was able to do. He did not need the Partition of Palestine to cause anti-Semitism to flourish in Germany and spread over the globe.

(Actually, the failure to carry out the U. N. decision for Partition may encourage anti-Semitism. Our scientific department tells us that the anti-Semite is essentially a sadistic person. The more he is convinced that the Jew is weak, the more he is stimulated in his anti-Semitism. Failure to achieve Partition, after it was voted by more than two-thirds of the United Nations, might be an overwhelming proof to the anti-Semite that the Jews are weak, powerless and uninfluential. This would encourage him to continue his anti-Semitic work.)

Jacob Blaustein's Speech, February 15, 1948.
Text that was discarded is in **bold** type on gray background.

So, again reminding you that I am not a prophet, I say (it, Partition) may increase our Civic Defense Problem here but I doubt it, at least to any material extent.

Here are some straws which may indicate the way anti-Semitism might, or might not, be affected by Partition. A Gallup poll of Americans (announced last November) showed that 65% of those questioned favored the proposed Partition plan. Only 10% were opposed; the remainder had no opinion.

Fine editorials have appeared in favor of implementation and enforcement of Partition in the country's leading newspapers - papers like our own Baltimore SUN, the New York Times, New York Herald Tribune. They do not treat with it as a Jewish issue. Their approach is from a United States and United Nations angle.

Of course, I do not say that if there is serious armed conflict between the Jews and the Arabs in Palestine and if United States soldiers, as part of a United States military force are hurt, that there may not be some repercussions here. But truth in the American press would un-doubtedly continue to stress that it is the Arabs, and not the Jews, who are taking the offensive in defiance of a decision of the United Nations, and that the very authority of this international body of which they themselves are members is being challenged by the Arabs. American Jews, together with their government, would be on the side of the United Nations, exactly as they sided with the democratic powers during the World Wars.

x - This is a different situation than before the United Nations decision when the (small) terrorist groups of Palestinian Jews took the offensive (and daily papers in this country carried headlines screaming of the King David Hotel explosions and hanging of a British sergeant even

Jacob Blaustein's Speech, February 15, 1948.
Text that was discarded is in **bold** type on gray background.

though it was British provocation. (y- If Partition fails, it is more than likely that these Jewish extremists will resort to terrorism and violence in spite of efforts to control them. (xx - It would also undoubtedly be made clear that this is not a 'Holy' war on the part of the Arabs - in a desire or effort of the Arab people (as such, themselves) - being war fostered by reactionary Moslems lead by the Grand Mufti of Jerusalem, Haj Amin el-Huseini, the notorious Nazi collaborator). Numerous declarations of friendship and good neighborliness have been made by Arab villages bordering Jewish Zones. Clearly the populace as a whole is opposed to strife.)

The thinking, however, of many authorities is that if the Security Council of the United Nations provides an international force, this in itself would have a quieting effect. That is also the opinion expressed in the Press such as in the New York Times editorial of February 4, 1948.

Further, I agree with the statement of Dr. Chaim Weizmann that when the states are established, means will be found for harmonious cooperation between the Jews and Arabs. The fact is that there have been many signs of friendship between native Arabs and native Jews. Indications include the mutual non-aggression pacts that have been entered into between quite a few Arab villages and Jewish colonies; and agreements by Arab villages adjacent to Jewish colonies not to shelter Arab attackers coming from outside Palestine. The populace as a whole is opposed to strife.

I should add that strong, non-sectarian organizations (like the American Association for the United Nations, service clubs such as the Kiwanis and Lions International, the American Federation of Labor, the Congress of Industrial Organizations,

Jacob Blaustein's Speech, February 15, 1948.
Text that was discarded is in **bold** type on gray background.

Railroad Brotherhoods and other labor unions, women's, farmer's and veterans' groups) are vigorously urging immediate lifting of the United States embargo on arms to Palestine and full American backing an international force and again, from the standpoint of the good of the United States and the United Nations.

The American people may well be sympathetic with the new Palestinian state because it will be a nation of pioneers in keeping with the pioneer traditions of America. The new state will be a democracy, as required by the U. N. resolution, and its constitution will likely be based on the American constitution. The whole history of America illustrates sympathy of our people with struggling young democracies of this sort.

B - I shall now list some other possible advantages which may be reflected by Partition to the (position, benefit) of the American Jew on what he has been aiming to accomplish on other fronts.

a - The (Jewish, Palestinian) state may be a safety valve for the future persecuted Jews throughout the world, and the American Jewish community might not have the same urge to exert constant pressure on the United States Government to protect Jews abroad.

(b - With pressure of furthering the Zionist aim for the establishment of a Jewish state in Palestine removed, the American Jew will be able to devote a considerable amount of time and energy towards deepening the social and cultural activities of his own community.)

c - The expected solution of the DP problem and the resulting lightening of the burden which the American Army in Germany is assuming today

Jacob Blaustein's Speech, February 15, 1948.
Text that was discarded is in **bold** type on gray background.

in regards to the DPs, may have a decided beneficial influence on the position of the Jews in the United States. The American taxpayer will not be called upon to spend millions of dollars for the care of Jewish DPs (among the others), and the Jewish organizations will not have to continue their pressure upon the government to provide for the DPs.
d. - Members of the American Army of Occupation are subjected to anti-Semitic influences at the present time. This will be largely removed with the disappearance of the DP problem.
e - The strained relationship between the Army and the DPs which creates a dangerous situation and which will likely increasingly affect public opinion in the United States will be removed.
(f - Reduction of funds necessary for maintainence of the DPs by the Army of Occupation would take place with the immigration of a large number of DPs to the (Jewish, Palestinian) state.)
g- With the large-scale immigration to the (Jewish, Palestinian) state, the liberalization of immigration to the United States may be much easier to accomplish. Unfortunately it appears that a large part of the opposition to the liberalization of immigration is due to the fact that there are Jews among them even though they represent only 20 of the total. Once the (Jewish, Palestinian) state is established, it will be more apparent - if it is a fact - that the Stratton Bill or any other bill in favor

Jacob Blaustein's Speech, February 15, 1948.
Text that was discarded is in **bold** type on gray background.

of the liberalization of immigration is 'not a Jewish Bill'.

h-Public opinion will not be subjected to daily headlines and advertisements in the newspapers with regards to the 'homelessness of the Jewish people'. Once the DP problem is settled Jews will cease to be a problem (?).

(i - Jews of Palestine will for a long time depend upon American Jewry for financial and other support. It is therefore likely that the official policy of the (Jewish, Palestinian) state will largely follow that of the United Nations.) *[Note: In context "United States" may have been meant.]*

(j - Economically, the Jewish state has a chance to develop and prosper only after it gains the sympathy and support of the United States and becomes, to a certain extent, an ? of the United States in the near East. Palestine, being the only modern community in the Near East, may in time become the headquarters of many American Companies and financial interests in that part of the world.) *[Question mark and space for word to be chosen, in original.]*

(k - The Jewish state will undoubtedly have to appeal to the United States and the International Bank of Reconstruction for funds. The influence of the United States will consequently be very great.)

(l - It is (most likely, assured) that the Constitution of the Jewish state, as well as its government, will be essentially democratic. The United Nations Partition Resolution itself imposes a democratic regime. A

natural affinity, therefore, may exist between the United States and the (Jewish, Palestinian) state based on the similarity of the constitutional principles. It is very likely that the American governmental structure will have a great influence upon that of the (Jewish, Palestinian) state.) (IV - In <u>my</u> opinion, (- and here I underscore my -), (American Jews should go along with the United Nations decision for Partition wholeheartedly. We have the responsibility of doing whatever we can toward the implementation of the Partition decision in a way that will minimize bloodshed in Palestine and keep low any harm to the position of the Jew in the United States. The following, I think should be the (attitude, position, course of conduct) of the American Jew.)

III - <u>NOW WHAT SHOULD BE THE POSITON OF THE AMERICAN JEW WITH REGARD TO THIS NEWLY TO-BE-CREATED STATE, AND WHAT SHOULD OUR COURSE OF CONDUCT BE?</u>

    1 - We, of course, want to continue to cooperate with Jews who live and wish to settle in Palestine. Its gates are now practically closed to that remnant of European Jewry which so eagerly wants to go there, and the new state is torn with violence and bloodshed, with the likelihood of more to come unless steps to prevent are taken.

        A - We, of course, cannot and must not do anything to aid them which would in any way constitute a violation of the laws or executive action of our country. That is definite. But we have a right, however, to remind our government that the United Nations did more than decide a dispute between two peoples. Through Partition, it set up a course of international conduct to help make for the peace of the world, and its decree must be supported - its

Jacob Blaustein's Speech, February 15, 1948.
Text that was discarded is in **bold** type on gray background.

mandate implemented. To enforce it, requires policing of Palestine against those Arabs who aim to sabotage the United Nations Resolution and thus strike at the very existence of the United Nations.

a - We therefore should continue to urge on the American government that it take the lead in the Security Council in advocating that the Council promptly take measures to create a constabulary and military force sufficient to maintain order in Palestine and repel external aggression. This international force should be created with dispatch. With the knowledge of its existence, it is quite possible that by conferences with the Arab aggressors, order can be made to prevail and progress assured. This, of course, would have to so within the framework of the Partition Plan. It appears that some of the Arab leaders, because of conflicting interests, are desirous of avoiding the struggle. But if any such conferences fail, the international force should act. If this force is not set up, the Arabs will interpret the omission as an encouragement of their fight against the U. N. Partition Plan.

(This international force might be composed of contingents supplied by the smaller powers not having a direct interest in Palestine. At the outset, regular soldiers might be required until volunteers are trained. Funds could be provided by the Big Nations, which might also have to give actual support in the event of external aggression. They would be under the commend of the United Nations, not of any single country. They would not represent individual states, but the organization as a whole. Or some other suitable formula should be devised. Haganah would, of course, do its part.)

b - <u>And this brings us to the debated question, shall we help arm Haganah?</u>

The mandatory power is not maintaining order in Palestine. The Arabs are threatening the peace and attempting to alter by force 'the settlement envisaged in the resolution'. The Mufti can obtain, and is obtaining, arms and men from other Arab states while Haganah cannot get arms. Haganah in Palestine is composed of Jews with the sole objective of defending their lives and homes and with it, the decision of the United Nations. They should be given the arms with which to make their defense effective.

    Haganah is to be the Jewish militia contemplated under the United Nations decree. Regardless of how we may have felt about a Jewish Army before this decision for Partition - and than were many Jews who disapproved of any such segregation within the armies of established countries in the last war - Haganah now is entitled to and must have our support and the means with which to carry on. The United Nations declared there should be two newly created states but thus far has provided no means of enforcement. What Haganah is attempting to do, therefore, is to enforce the United Nations decision. That is legitimate and essential.

    We should continue to urge the United States to lift the embargo on the export of arms to Palestine to the extent of permitting such arms to be exported under the direction of the Security Council or the U. N. Commission.

c - We should continue to urge the United States to use its good offices to secure from the mandatory power, Britain, the cooperation intended under the terms of the United Nations resolution, such as agreeing for the U. N. Commission to go to Palestine forthwith, cooperation in setting up the specified militia and opening up promptly a free port for Jewish immigration.

d - The position outlined above to be taken with our government is not just a Jewish position. It is a pro-American and a pro-United Nations position. It in a position which all right-thinking Americans, Jews or non-Jews, can support.

e - <u>Now what are some of the questions which must be decided in connection with the new state?</u> The American Jewish Committee expects to follow through with the Jewish Agency on various situations. We have already informed the Jewish Agency that the name, the constitution and the governmental system that will be established in Palestine are important to all Jews and the Committee has assurances from leaders of the Jewish Agency - repeated to Judge Proskauer and me last week - that we will be fully consulted with respect to these. The United Nations, of course, has the primary responsibility carefully to scrutinize the constitution and governmental system phases.

As to the name, it appears to me now that 'The Jewish State' or 'Judea', for obvious reasons, would be undesirable. The name 'New Judea' might be somewhat better. The name 'Eretz Israel' has been considered. Perhaps the name 'Zion' would be preferable.

As to the constitution, it must be democratic and based on a Bill of Rights without any link between Church and State. Arabs and Christians, representing minorities, must be assured equal rights in fact as well as in theory. A constitutional system must be devised, preferably modeled on the American Presidential System.

The Jewish Agency, set up under the provisions of the British Mandate, should go out of existence shortly after the new state actually comes unto being, handing its functions over to the provisional government of state.

It seems to me that Zionist organizations throughout the world and Zionist organizations in America will have no more of their original function and could be dissolved. Their ultimate aim will have been achieved.

The former divisions into Zionists, non-Zionists and anti-Zionists could the[n] probably disappear. The Jews in America could create an organization like the 'American Friends of Palestine' or of the final name of the country, which would be a non-political agency with activities limited to securing material and moral support for the newly created state. Jews in other countries could do likewise. Various segments of the Jewish community, irrespective of their previous political attitude toward Zionism, might join this organization, and friction be greatly diminished.

f - Any attempt at political identification between the Jews in America and the newly created state must be fought vigorously. We must continue to make definitely clear in all quarters that we are against World Nationalism.

g - To repeat a previous point, we must continue to assert, if and when the question arises, that we American Jews do not have a dual allegiance. In the main, the charge will be by propagandists - the work of anti-Semites.

h - I wish our anti-Zionist friends would realize that expositions given out to the general public implying that a large number of the Jews in the United Status have, or may, put their allegiance to the new state in Palestine parallel with or over their allegiance to the United States, are playing right into the hands of anti-Semites. Refraining from this, of course, would not preclude free speech on this topic among our own groups.

i - American Jews must never act, nor give the false impression, that we are a single political unit. Thus, in my opinion, the idea of an organization like the American Jewish Assembly which, according to its plan, among other things, 'in the field of international affairs shall act for American Jewry in all representations before the United States government and its departments, intergovernmental agencies and the United Nations' is badly conceived. It might give the erroneous impression that it has the authority to speak as one for American Jews. There is no single spokesman for American Jewry, nor can there be.

There is a big difference between this concept and unity of action wherever possible of separate, unrelated organizations within the areas of their own agreements.

j - Now, there are a number of additional things which I think American Jews should do and continue to do. Time permits I mention only two of them briefly.

Palestine must not be the sole haven for displaced Jews. We must continue to strive for enlarged immigration opportunities into other countries and particularly into the United States advancing both the 'humanitarian' reasons and the 'American interest' reasons. Though a very large proportion of the displaced Jews have expressed a desire for Palestine, there are a number whose eyes turn hopefully elsewhere and especially towards the United States. With a possibility of large-scale immigration to the new Palestinian state, the liberalization of immigration to the United States - through the passage of the Stratton bill or similar bill - may be much easier to accomplish.

We must also continue to work, as the American Jewish Committee is doing, for the improvement of the situation in Europe for those Jews who do not wish to go to Palestine or to the United States or elsewhere. There are some who wish to stay in the lands of their fathers and try to pick up once more the thread of their interrupted existence.

IV - CONCLUSION.

In conclusion, I would like to venture an observation. It applies not only to the Jews remaining in Europe but for Jews in Palestine and elsewhere. It is this. Relief, though vitally important; is not enough. Even restitution of confiscated property for which the American Jewish Committee has worked in Europe is not enough, though that is essential. These are the necessary means for restoring life and means of livelihood.

But that life and that livelihood will be tragically unavailing unless the entire spiritual and mental climate is changed so that Jews will be able to function freely and with respect and dignity.

Jacob Blaustein's Speech, February 15, 1948.
Text that was discarded is in **bold** *type on gray background.*

It is more than mere safety of the body that we must demand and support (financially in our campaigns and otherwise), necessary as that is; it is safety of the soul that we are seeking. In such a program, Palestine Partition plays an important role.

I. The American Jewish Committee, the Zionist Organization & the Balfour Declaration

*Jewish village Mazkeret Batya in Palestine, founded 1883.
(Photo: Leo Kahan, Yidishe Zeitung, Vienna, 1912.)*

Organize, Organize, Organize, until every Jew in America must stand up and be counted, counted with us, or prove himself, wittingly or unwittingly, of the few who are against their own people.[52]

Louis D. Brandeis (1915)

The Zionistic propaganda has heretofore had the futility of a mirage; at this juncture it has the peril of a menace.[53]

Prof. Jacob H. Hollander (1918)

"Much enthusiasm among our down-town co-religionists."

The AJC was founded in 1906 by prominent and successful German-Jewish Americans — men who were not of the recent wave of eastern European Jews that had made New York City "the largest centre of Jewish population in the world."[54] The 1907 annual meeting of the committee was held at the Hotel Astor, and officers included such eminent men as Cyrus Adler, Louis Marshall, Mayer Sulzberger, Julian Mack, Isaac W. Bernheim, Judah Magnes, and Cyrus L. Sulzberger.

The creation of the Committee was an American Jewish response to the Kishinev massacres and other pogroms.[55] The 1906 letter from Louis Marshall proposing the formation of the AJC cited "the necessity of extending to our brethren, a helping hand in a manner most conducive to the accomplishment of a permanent improvement of their unfortunate condition...as long as the objects of our solicitude are subjected to disabilities and persecution, owing to their religious belief."

The letter from Marshall anticipated "if such a Committee be organized, it shall be on lines as shall not only meet with the approval of

---

52 Louis D. Brandeis, "The Jewish Problem: How To Solve It," Speech to the Conference of Eastern Council of Reform Rabbis, April 25, 1915, www.law.louisville.edu/library/collections/brandeis/node/234
53 See page 70.
54 "Jewish Committee Meets," November 11, 1907, NY Times, page 16.
55 "FROM KISHINEFF TO BIALYSTOK. A TABLE OF POGROMS FROM 1903 TO 1906," American Jewish Year Book Vol. 8 (1906-1907), page 34-89. Extensive report summarizing locations and circumstances of attacks against Jewish people and communities in the Russian empire.

the general [both Jewish and gentile] public, but shall be free from all objectionable tendencies."[56]

This contrasts with the backbone of American Jewish Zionist support, which thrived with the highly politicized zest of Eastern European tumult, where labor organizing, for instance, was done in a "Jewish" context, as in the Jewish Labor Bund in Russia/Poland, or the Workmen's Circle (Arbeter Ring) among new immigrants in the United States.[57]

The AJC, as well as the later anti-Zionist organization American Council for Judaism(ACJ), fought its association, in the minds of American Jews, with assimilation and complacency.

(Years later, in 1958, the American Council for Judaism hired the Washington Public Opinion Laboratory (WPOL) of the University of Washington Department of Sociology in Seattle to answer the question how the ACJ could increase membership of American Jews — conducting "a three year study in depth, of the human values and attitudes involved in the relationship between American Jews, their faith and the American environment."[58]

(The WPOL report concluded that the ACJ mostly appealed to assimilated western European/German American Jews, and since they were greatly outnumbered in the US Jewish population by more recent immigrants of eastern European origin, its prospects as an organization were dim.[59])

The tone of the first sentence of this 1888 news article of a Lower East Side meeting of Hovevei Zion in the English-language *American Hebrew* magazine may give a flavor of the division between established "German-American" Jews and eastern European newcomers:

---

56 Louis Marshall, "Letter calling for a meeting to discuss the establishment of the American Jewish Committee," January 8, 1906, ajcarchives.org.
57 See Rabbi Philipson's testimony, page 66.
58 Rabbi Elmer Berger to Lewis L. Strauss, February 10, 1958, Admiral Lewis Lichtenstein Strauss Papers; P-632; box 1; folder 1; AJHS.
59 "Evidence from a variety of research procedures converges on the conclusion that a major function of the A.C.J. for the largest share of its members is to protest the erosion of their identity as integrated Jews in the classical Reform, German-Jewish tradition..." "Final Report on Project Concord, Part Three: Evidence Regarding Influences that Have Shaped the Attitudes of Members and non-Members," (U:60-121), box 13, folder 4, accession no. 05-024 Sociology Dept. (Project Concord ACJ), University of Washington Libraries Special Collections, Seattle.

Admirers of Zion.

The public meeting of the Admirers of Zion, held on Sunday last at 177 East Broadway, provided that the idea of Palestinian colonization is creating much enthusiasm among our down-town co-religionists. The rather spacious meeting hall was nearly overcrowded and the audience a very lively interest in the proceedings of the evening. The meeting was opened by Mr. A. Derenberg, the President of the Society. He gave a brief account of the Society's workings since its two years of existence, and read reports from various colonies in Palestine, showing that but comparatively little outside assistance was needed to make these colonies self-supporting. Rev. Dr. B. Drachman was the first speaker, and made a warm-hearted and earnest appeal for the Society. Rev. Dr. Zinsler next aroused the audience to a high pitch of enthusiasm by his fiery and eloquent references to the love that every Jewish heart bears towards Zion and Jerusalem. Dr. G. Lieberman made some very thoughtful and much applauded remarks on the great importance of the ever-living Jewish question, which can find its only proper solution in the direction of such undertakings as this Society has engaged in. Hon. Judge Henry M. Goldfogle, who was given a rousing reception, then addressed the audience, praising in happy words the objects of the Society and its eminent usefulness. The meeting was enclosed with an interesting address by Rev. Mr. Brodsky. Over sixty joined the Society as new members, and there is good prospects that the membership of the Society will grow rapidly hereafter. All desiring to join are requested to communicate with A. Rosenberg, 132 Nassau Street, or J.I. Bluestone, 172 Madison Street.[60]

---

60 American Hebrew, May 11, 1888, page 15. Presumably "J.I. Bluestone" was future Federation of American Zionists co-founder I.J. Bluestone.

Before Balfour / Ottoman Palestine

LEADERS OF the AJC were well involved in the welfare of the small Jewish population in Ottoman Palestine.

A 1912 letter in AJC files from Dina (Mrs. Nathan) Straus in Jerusalem testifies to the visit and involvement of Nathan Straus — brother of the AJC's Oscar S. Straus. Nathan was a lifelong philanthropist of Palestine, and is namesake of the Israeli city of Natanya. The letter mentions that Dr. and Mrs. Judah Magnes are in Jaffa.[61]

With the onset of the Great War in 1914, the AJC and the Federation of American Zionists (FAZ; later Zionist Organization of America) jointly funded a US State Department / Navy delivery of $50,000 to Jews in Palestine:

> *Toward the end of August, the Committee received urgent cablegrams from the hon. Henry Morgenthau, the United States Ambassador to Turkey, stating that the Jews of Palestine were facing a terrible crisis, that destruction threatened the thriving colonies, and that at least the sum of fifty thousand dollars was immediately required to relieve the situation, which was described as really pitiable, that a responsible committee, headed by Dr. Arthur Ruppin, had prepared a plan for the establishment of a loan fund for the relief of the distress caused by the war.*
>
> *At the meeting held on August 31, 1914, your Committee after a thorough discussion of the situation, resolved that the exigency warranted the appropriation of a substantial sum from the Emergency Trust Fund. Upon the generous offer of Mr. Jacob H. Schiff to contribute one fourth of the $50,000 required, the Committee voted a contribution of twenty-five thousand dollars, and invited the Federation of American Zionists to contribute the further sum of twelve thousand five hundred dollars to complete the sum required. That organization responded, turning over the required sum to the Committee.*[62]

---

61 Letter from "Dina" to "My dear Oscar," March 21, 1912, General Correspondence 1906-1932, box 16, folder Palestine 1912-1928, AJC.
62 "Activities of the American Jewish Committee During the Year 1914," 4 page mimeograph, Papers of Louis Marshall; P-24; box 1; folder 14; AJHS.

Palestine was only one part of AJC activities to aid Jews abroad. In the same year, AJC gave $100,000 to help establish the American Jewish Relief Committee for Sufferers from the War (later part of JDC); coordinated with the Anglo-Jewish Association, Alliance Israelite Universale, and Israelitische Allianz of Vienna, to aid Jews of Europe caught in the war; and continued their perennial efforts to protect the rights and lives of Jews in Eastern European nations such as Moldova and Romania.

Finding safety and better lives for Jews in distress abroad was a preoccupation of American Jewish communal leaders. Cyrus Adler was involved in the founding of the American Federation of the Jewish Territorial Organization in 1906, and was Chairman of the Industrial Removal Office.[63] (The Industrial Removal Office attempted to settle Jewish immigrants from eastern Europe away from the great concentrations of Jews in tenement life in NY and in the northeast.)

Domestically, AJC fought immigration restrictions, and for enforcement of the 1913 New York State Civil Rights Act for Public Accommodations.[64] It also continued the production of the community mainstay American Jewish Year Book, which it had assumed from the Jewish Publication Society.

A March 28, 1915 3-page letter from Samuel Edelman[65], on stationary of American Consulate, Jerusalem, to Louis Marshall "in accordance with your request to give you information about Palestine from time to time," reports "the safety of Jews in Palestine is assured" currently, and reviews the trying economic and political circumstances of life there. In writing about planning for after the war, he recommends to Marshall the "necessity of Internationalizing Palestine":

"From the Jewish point of view it is absolutely essential; and has the warm support of local Zionist leaders (like Dr. Ruppin), in contrast to the usual utterings of some of the Zionist leaders now in America, whose remarks on this subject has (sic) been brought to my attention. No one nation will be able to give complete economic and political independence to the subjects of the country without necessarily favoring some one group, which is

---

63 *American Jewish Yearbook*, Vol. 8 (1906-07), pages 106 and 114.
64 Jeffrey Gurock, "New York State Civil Rights Act," Association for Jewish Studies (AJS) *Review*, Vol. 1 (1976), pp. 93-120.
65 American Vice Consul at Aleppo. *FRUS, 1915, Supplement, The World War,* page VIII.

bound to cause a good deal of ill feeling and discontent.... I have urged this proposition upon Mr. Oscar Straus and I hope you will give it your earnest attention.[66]

---

66 Samuel Edelman to Louis Marshall, March 28, 1915, General Correspondence 1906-1932, box 16, folder Palestine 1912-1928, AJC.

"The general impression appears to be that the Shomerim are innocent of aggression."

In 1915, Henrietta Szold reported from Palestine the elements that from the start would make for armed alienation between communities.

Palestine was a Turkish province, Szold explained:

> In Turkey a certain degree of autonomy is granted to ethnographic, national, and religious groups. Hence the severance of nationalities and religious communities from each other in their peculiar "quarters" in the cities is more marked than in most countries, and hence we have the internal government of the Jewish rural and city communities.

Turkish Palestine administration reinforced "separate" development of different groups. In the Jewish settlements, there was a colonial, garrison quality to life.

> From the first it was necessary to guard against depredations by the Arabs, and watchmen were engaged from among the suspects to patrol the Jewish fields at night.... In the winter of 1909-1910, dissatisfaction with the prevailing system was rife. Especially in the Galilean highland, the nursery of Jewish sentiment from of old, the more ardent spirits among the young workingmen could not brook the humiliation the Jewish farmers had to endure. Word flew from settlement to settlement, and the Jewish colony guard came into existence....
> In spite of the costliness of the service, there seems to be hardly a dissenting voice as to its value, a recognition the more remarkable as the citizen, the Baale-Battim, element in the villages still squirms at the idea of a self-constituted and self-governed company of Jewish youths, revolver armed, most of them noted for zeal and ebullient enthusiasm. That the discharged Arab guard looks upon Shomerim as "scabs" is not calculated to allay anxiety. The situation offers redoubtable openings on both sides, and there have been a few bloody, even fatal encounters between the two nationalities. The general impression appears to be that the Shomerim are innocent of aggression; they have gone to extremes only in self-defense. Besides insuring the safety of Jewish property,

> *Ha-Shomer has raised the dignity of the Jew in the eyes
> of his Arab neighbors....
> At all events, Ha-Shomer with its hundred
> and more members has become an absolute necessity in
> Palestine, and a picturesque feature in its rural life. The
> company is made up of the material needed for the
> pioneer bands that are to prepare outlying regions
> through occupancy by themselves for permanent
> settlement and cultivation by others.*[*]

Discussing early (1882-1899) attempts at colonization, Szold remarks there were many failures.

> *Some of them did not even shrink from hiring themselves
> out as farm help to the Arabs in the neighboring villages.*

Szold's comment illustrates that, although emigrés to a new country in hard times would of course hire out to established farmers, to Zionists in Palestine creation of a homeland meant economic fraternization was unusual. Later, Histadrut, the Zionist labor syndicate, ran enterprises with the policy of only using "Hebrew labor."

Szold recounts the growth of the Jewish orange industry, which would create export enterprises bypassing established Arab channels. The logic of this was economic, but the impact of this lack of integration to existing Palestinian life can be imagined.

> *In the early days the Jewish orange-growers were
> wholly dependent on the Arab dealers in Jaffa, who
> monopolized the foreign trade. The Jewish growers were
> thus not in a position to shape the trade conditions, the
> camel transportation to the port, the shipments, and the
> sales. Through co-operation the Jewish growers
> established their own sales-agencies abroad, secured
> control over shipping facilities and wharf privileges, and
> so lessened the expenses and increased the profits of the
> growers considerably. Latterly a second such
> organization, the Union, has been formed. The inspection
> of the fruit and its packing for the foreign markets have
> improved under the co-operative system...*[67]

---

[*] Zionists decisions in Palestine were made in the philosophy of "Negation of the Diaspora," *shlilat ha'galut*, consciously "remaking" a new sort of Jew. Ben Gurion reacted to hiring Arab guards in Ottoman Palestine by writing, "Was it conceivable that here too we should be deep in Galuth, hiring strangers to guard our property and protect our lives?" David Ben Gurion, *Rebirth and Destiny of Israel*, Philosophical Library, New York, 1954, page 14.

[67] Henrietta Szold, "Recent Jewish Progress in Palestine," AJYB, 1915-1916, pages 89,

A Conference or a Congress?

A PRECURSOR conflict between the Federation of American Zionists (FAZ, later the Zionist Organization of America) and the AJC was fought in 1915.

The issue was the calling of a representative "Jewish Congress" in America, in response to the crisis for Jews of the European war. The AJC executive committee had resolved on June 20, 1915,
> *That a Conference be held of delegates from Jewish national societies throughout the country, for the sole purpose of considering the Jewish question as it affects our brethren in belligerent lands;*
> *THAT the number of delegates to this Conference shall not exceed one hundred and fifty...*[68]

Zionists protested the limited scope of the conference and demanded a "representative Congress" on Jewish issues. This issue would recur, with the AJC contesting the claim of Stephen S. Wise's American Jewish Congress to represent American Jews as a polity.[69][70]

On July 22, 1915, Louis Lipsky of the FAZ wrote a "Dear Comrade" letter to Zionists calling for all-out public protests against the AJC:
> *The status of our negotiations with the American Jewish Committee in our attempt to secure unity of action on the Jewish Congress issue, makes it necessary that throughout the United States a public demonstration be made expressive of the feelings of American Jews with regard to this important question. It is desirable and urgent that every Zionist use his influence to call local conferences, mass meetings, etc., to have resolutions*

94-95, 39, 57.
68 American Jewish Committee Minutes Vol. III, Executive Committee, June 20, 1915 - Dec. 9, 1917, page 311, AJC.
69 "As Americans and as Jews we are not willing to give any man or men control over Jewish Affairs." Editorial, *American Hebrew*, Vol. 143, No. 5, June 17, 1938, pp 3-4. "Dr. Wise devoted fifty-five of a sixty-minute talk...to a personal and slanderous attack upon [AJC's] Dr. Cyrus Adler....this has been, without question, the greatest propaganda drive ever conducted in Jewish life. It has been as unremitting and as carefully planned to deaden all sensibilities as any Hitler propaganda drive ever was."
70 In 1948, Blaustein wrote Proskauer, "Like you, I am deeply concerned over the concept of the World Jewish Congress that it speak for all Jews everywhere (based on which, incidentally, it has been trying to get special consultant status for itself before the U.N.)." Blaustein to Proskauer, July 12, 1948, Box 2.21,file C-2-23 Proskauer, Judge Joseph M., JHU.

> adopted ENDORSING UNEQUIVOCALLY THE
> RESOLUTION OF THE PROVISIONAL COMMITTEE
> ADOPTED AT BOSTON, in effect:
>
> THAT A JEWISH CONGRESS BE HELD, CALLED
> JOINTLY BY JEWISH ORGANIZATIONS, AND
> ORGANIZAED ON a democratic basis, which shall
> discuss the whole Jewish problem in all its phases;
>
> THAT NO LIMITED CONFERENCE CAN TAKE THE
> PLACE OF SUCH A CONGRESS, AND THAT SHOULD
> SUCH A LIMITED CONFERENCE BE HELD, IT WOULD
> NOT BE REPRESENTATIVE OF THE SENTIMENTS
> AND DESIRES OF THE JEWS OF AMERICA.
>
> We appeal to you to use all your energies during the next
> few weeks to secure such an expression of opinion from
> your community, and that you aid in having that opinion
> given the widest and most effective publicity.[71]

Cyrus Adler of the AJC wrote FAZ president Louis Brandeis,
> I do not believe that, pending negotiations upon which
> we entered in all loyalty and with the fullest desire to
> bring about cooperation, you have sanctioned a
> policy...to bring about a series of agitations throughout
> the country aiming to influence these negotiations. I feel
> sure you will have this action disavowed.[72]

Magnes, negotiating with the Provisional Executive Committee of the FAZ, reported that "if we (the AJC) are not able to reach an agreement with the Zionists, a number of the (other Jewish) organizations will decline to sign the invitation with us, and we would thus be laying ourselves over to refusals on their part to cooperate."[73]

Rabbi Jacob Kohn of Temple Ansche Chesed in Harlem wrote Lipsky of the FAZ, "It is my firm conviction that the Zionist Organization in disdaining the invitation sent it by the American Jewish Committee and in taking part in the agitation for the so-called democratic Congress, has

---

71 American Jewish Committee Minutes Vol. III, Executive Committee, June 20, 1915 - Dec. 9, 1917, page 352, AJC.
72 Page 353, *ibid.*
73 Page 355, *ibid.*

deliberately put itself on the side of schism and disunion in American Jewish affairs, without securing for Zionism any substantial gain."[74]

A meeting of Presidents of National Jewish Organizations was ultimately "called by Mr. Adolph Kraus, President of the Independent Order B'nai B'rith" on Oct. 3, 1915, in New York. AJC President Louis Marshall reported

The meeting... was held at the Hotel Astor at 10:30 A.M., and was in practically continuous session until 7 P.M. ... All who spoke at the meeting were of the opinion that the appointed time the Jews of the country should through concerted action, place before the proper authorities, national or international as may be deemed best, their basic demands that the Jews be accorded equal civil, political and religious rights in countries where they are now oppressed.[75]

On July 21, the executive committee had discussed a proposed conference of Jews from neutral countries.

The CHAIRMAN presented the summary of the letter received by Dr. Magnes from Dr. Alexander Marmoreck of Zurich. Dr. Marmoreck stated that the Jews of Switzerland are expecting to take the initiative in calling a conference of the representatives of Jews of neutral lands for the purpose of discussing all of the implications of the Jewish question in Europe. Mr. (Jacob) SCHIFF was of the opinion that the Committee should adhere to its policy, at least for the present, of refraining from any

---

74 Jacob Kohn to Louis Lipsky, August 24, 1915, Papers of Louis Lipsky 1873-1963, P-672, box 1, file 4, AJHS.
75 Page 379, *ibid*. "Those present at the Conference were: Adolph Kraus and A. B. Seelenfreund, Independent Order B'nai B'rith; Cyrus Adler, United Synagogue; William Rosenau, Central Conference of American Rabbis; Samuel Dorf, Order B'rith Abraham; J. Walter Freiberg, Union of American Hebrew Congregations; Simon Miller, Jewish Publication Society; Oscar S. Straus, American Jewish Historical Society; Dr. Solomon Schechter, Jewish Theological Seminary of America; Emil Tausig, Independent Order Free Sons of Israel; A. D. Katcher, Federation of Galician and Bukowinian Jews; Leon Sanders, Independent Order B'rith Abraham; Louis Marshall, American Jewish Committee; Dr. Louis S. Rubinsohn, Independent Order B'rith Shalom; Dr. Harry Friedenwald, Federation of American Zionists; Dr. Solomon Diamont, Federation of Roumanian Jews; Rev. Dr. Bernard Drachman, Union of Orthodox Congregations; Dr. I. J. Bluestone, Mizrachi; M.Z. Margolies, Union of Orthodox Rabbis; Dr. Frank Rosenblatt, Arbeiter Ring; Judge Julian W. Mack, National Council of Young Men's Hebrew Associations; Louis D. Brandeis, Zionist Provisional Committee; Jacob Karlinger, Federation of Russian-Polish Hebrews of America."

open alliances or conferences with the representatives of European Jews. The Jews of the United States live in such different political conditions from the Jews of Europe, that any such action on our part would be misconstrued. The CHAIRMAN said that in his opinion our stand ought to be that we are preparing ourselves to have a conference among our own organizations in the fall, and that after we have had such a conference, we will be in a better position to say what course we deem best. In the meantime, a conference of the Jews of the so-called neutral nations is considered inadvisable.

Mr. (Oscar S.) STRAUS thought that it would not be well to say that we consider such a conference inadvisable, but that we do consider it unwise for citizens of the United States to join in such a conference. After all, we must bear in mind that whatever we will be able to do in this country, will have to be ultimately through Government. We must regulate ourselves by American conditions and American actions in this country.[76]

---

[76] Page 345, AJC minutes, *ibid.*

"The American Jews stand united"

After the war, an American Jewish Congress was finally convened in Philadelphia in December 1918.

The Congress endorsed "the development of Palestine into a Jewish commonwealth," the New York Times reported, and
> *delegates and visitors...jumped to their feet with shouts of joy in the feeling that their age-long dream of a homeland for their people was soon to be an accomplished fact.*
> *The members of the congress joined in singing the official Zionist song, "Hatik Voh," while a delegate jumped on the stage and waved the Stars and Stripes and the blue and white Jewish flag. The delegates embraced each other, and with tears of joy.*

The Palestine resolution mirrored the Balfour Declaration, with a clause, "it being clearly understood that nothing shall be done which shall prejudice the civil and religious rights of existing non-Jewish communities in Palestine or the rights and political status enjoyed by Jews in any other country."

A controversy arose over the American gathering calling for convening a World Jewish Congress (WJC), with a delegate saying the decision "will bring on it the well deserved criticism of a sober world." The issue of the American Jewish Congress and WJC claiming representative status for Jews was ever contentious.[77]

Congress chairman Judge Julian Mack said the Congress' actions "are <u>an acceptance on behalf of American Jewry</u> of the opportunities for the Jewish people that have been offered by Great Britain in the Balfour Declaration."[78]

The congress chose a delegation to attend the Versailles peace conference to present its "bill of rights" for the Jews of the world, led by Julian Mack and including Louis Marshall, Rabbi Stephen S. Wise, and Jacob de Haas. The list of items to be in the constitutions of new states

---

77 See page 59n.
78 "Adopts Palestine as Jews' Homeland," New York Times, December 18, 1918, page 24. Emphasis added.

created after the war included rights of "minority representation" as national groups.[79]

At the end of the congress, chairman and Zionist leader Mack claimed unanimity. "We have had our differences and have fought them out,' he declared. 'The American Jews stand united.'"[80]

A few days subsequently, the New York Times published a letter and an article (formerly an extended letter to his congressman Rollin B. Sanford) opposing the Congress' actions, from Simon W. Rosendale, former New York State Attorney General. The letter began,
> *In view of the pretentious Jewish organization, originating in Austria[*], known as "Zionism," and of the recent holding of a "Congress" in Philadelphia...it may be of interest to know that there is a large body of Jews who dissent from and are opposed to the movement....May I be pardoned for practically herein repeating the substance of that letter [to Rep. Sanford], as publication...will assist in laying before the public the fact that American citizens of Jewish faith are by no means united in approval of these activities."*

Rosendale reviewed the Reform movement's historic opposition to Zionism:
> *Their religion is concerned with the State only to the same extent to which all other denominations share the common aim of praying working for the highest welfare of one's native or adopted country. But the implications of a Jewish Palestine State include those distasteful, dangerous, and outworn doctrines of a combination of Church and State from the evils of which the world is being more and more saved, hence they neither participate in, nor approve of, the efforts to establish a Jewish Palestine State....*
>
> *It goes without saying that any effort to provide a place where oppressed or persecuted Jews may find a place to live in peace, as well as any movement toward educational or cultural advancement, must meet with universal approval.*
>
> *Thus, if the British declaration had been for a free*

---
79 See Jacob Blaustein's June 1945 comments on "national rights," page 123.
80 "Jews Going to Paris with Bill of Rights," New York Times, Dec. 19, 1918, page 8.
* Theodor Herzl was an Austro-Hungarian citizen.

> State, open for all with protection to all, no such question could be raised, but this is very different from, and issue is taken on, the proposition to establish Jewish nationality.[81]

Establishing the claim of the representative character for American Jews of the 1,000 delegates from major Jewish organizations, and of the congress' decisions, was prominent in Louis Lipsky's 1922 testimony to the U.S. House Foreign Affairs Committee hearings on a resolution on "Establishment of a National Home in Palestine."

Lipsky told the House committee that 360,000 American Jews had participated in selecting delegates from American Jewish organizations to attend. The Palestine resolution had begun, "The American Jewish Congress, speaking for the Jews of America..."[82]

Rep. Hamilton Fish, the sponsor of the House resolution endorsing the League of Nations British Palestine Mandate to implement the Balfour declaration, told the committee, "Palestine, the ancient homeland of the Jew, is to-day a comparatively sterile country...a devastated and sparsely settled land."[83]

Professor Edward Bliss Reed of New Haven, Connecticut, told the committee "The reason that I do not want your vote for this resolution is because it is absolutely un-American" in that it ignored the rights of Palestinian Arabs. He told the committee, "The Arabs, who form 93 per cent of the population, are decidedly disaffected. They complain of a gross injustice being done to them," and quoted from Shibly Jamal, secretary of the Arab Palestinian delegation in London, asking for a government inquiry before the Mandate for Palestine was implemented,

> Certain hurried commitments were made in 1917 to the Zionist organization, which have not conducted to peace and happiness in Palestine....
> The Palestine Arab delegation, therefore, appeals to the British government...to reserve their decision on the mandate until an investigation has found out the truth.
> A hurried settlement that is not based on the recognition of the facts must inevitably lead to disaster. The ideal must be realized through channels of the real.

---
81 "Americanism vs. Zionism," New York Times, Dec. 22, 1918, page 40.
82 "Establishment of a National Home in Palestine," Hearings Before the Committee on Foreign Affairs, House of Representatives, 67th Congress 2nd Session, on H.Con.Res 52, April 18, 19, 20, and 21, 1922, GPO, page 4.
83 Page 2, *ibid*.

> *The Arab population of Palestine is a fact, and should be the main concern of politicians who are rearranging the world. To ignore this fact of the Arabs in Palestine and their unwillingness to be dominated by political Zionism may succeed for a while with the help of British armored cars and airplanes.*[84]

Rabbi David Philipson, of Cincinnati, Ohio, brought the anti-Zionist Jewish message to the committee, telling them,

> *There are those of us who feel that Jewish nationalism does not express the true interpretation of Judaism. We feel Judaism is a religion, and that we are nationals of the country in which we are born and in which we live.*
>
> *That is the decided opinion of quite a large number of Jews....*

Philipson posited that the group conception of Jews meant bringing "the east European attitude to America... Bringing the group thought and the group idea into America from those countries where the Jews are forced to be a group minority....the state of mind that the Jews are a separate group, a separate national group."[85]

---

84 Page 72, *ibid.*
85 Page 100, *ibid.*

"WE CANNOT BLINK THE FACT NOR LEAVE THE WHOLE SUBJECT TO THE ZIONISTS."

AJC PRESIDENT Louis Marshall and the Executive Committee began considering a response to British (Balfour) Declaration at its Jan. 13, 1918 meeting, and considered it at three more meetings, before approving a statement for the general membership April 10. The statement was approved at a special AJC meeting April 28, 1918.[86]

Marshall said: "We cannot blink the fact nor leave the whole subject to the Zionists. There is the status of all the Jews of the world which may be affected by the action taken on this subject. It may be of the utmost importance to us that we make some sort of declaration, defining our position, indicating how far we are to go. This problem may affect not only the few who may go to Palestine, but also the millions who will never go to Palestine. It is essential that we should not ignore the problem but meet it"[87]

At the Feb. 2 meeting, Marshall presented the following news report of a statement made by star historian Prof. Albert Bushnell Hart of Harvard University:

"[Hart]...declared that Jews either have to renounce their citizenship or else have to give up Zionism....

"Zionism is a dangerous doctrine, and is bound to be given up sooner or later by the Jewish people".[88]

In response to a survey of AJC chapters done by the Executive Committee, Isaac W. Bernheim sent a statement to the Feb. meeting:

To becloud the title to his American citizenship by creating the impression that he is only a sojourner in this land; that he is ready when the proper moment will have arrived to transfer his allegiance to a foreign land is in my humble opinion nothing short of a crime towards those rugged pioneers and their descendants who by their wholehearted and un-selfish devotion to their fatherland succeeded in securing for the American Israelite, proper recognition and the fullest opportunities politically and otherwise.

---

86 AJYB, Vol. 20 (1918-19), page 406-407.
87 February 2, 1918 meeting, MINUTES VOL. IV EXECUTIVE COMMITTEE Jan. 13, 1918 - May 27, 1923, page 639, AJC.
88 Minutes report it as from the February 1, 1918 edition of *American Hebrew*. Clipping is in file "Palestine 1912-28 ," General Correspondence 1906-1932., box 16, AJC.

> *I most respectfully urge that the Executive Committee keep to the middle of the road, abstaining from endorsing or supporting a movement fraught with the gravest consequences to American Israel.*[89]

Zionist Julian Mack pushed for clarity in the AJC position:
> *If we agree and if some of our members agree with Prof. Hart, and I think Mr. Bernheim on first thought would agree with him -- if in our judgment, those who agree with Prof. Hart are wrong, then we should make it perfectly clear that they are wrong. That is due to our constituency.*[90]

In the 1918 discussion, Magnes illustrates the distinction being drawn by the AJC between upbuilding a "Jewish homeland" in Palestine, and supporting a Jewish political entity there:
> *The whole question has two aspects. One is the political aspect and the other is that of the actually building up of the country. It seems to me that these two aspects have to be kept apart. The political aspect is the chief concern of the Zionist organization....The question before the American Jewish Committee and before all other Jews outside the Zionist Organization is an entirely different one. It is the question of helping to build up Palestine after the war is over...*[91]

The minutes continue,
> Dr. [Cyrus] ADLER stated that he agrees with Dr. Magnes' view as to the lack of finality of the Balfour letter....
> Dr. ADLER said further that he did not believe that the Jewish people have a legal claim to Palestine. The whole course of the world history shows that when a people have removed to other lands for 2,000 years, whether voluntarily or involuntarily, their legal right to the land is gone. He shared the Jewish hope of the restoration of Palestine. Whether it be as an independent state or under English or Turkish sovereignty, Palestine is sacred and should be for those Jews who want to go to Palestine to practice Judaism.

---

89 February 2, 1918 meeting, MINUTES VOL. IV EXECUTIVE COMMITTEE Jan. 13, 1918 - May 27, 1923, page 629, AJC.
90 Page 639, *ibid*.
91 Page 641, *ibid*.

> *One of the by-products of the Balfour declaration which is very distasteful is the statement that has been frequently made that the Jewish people will be given an opportunity to go back to Palestine and to live side by side with the newly organized Arab nationality and the Armenian people. It is difficult to imagine how Jews, who have lived in the great world, in the great modern cities of Europe and America, and who should go back to Palestine, could take a place side by side with the Arabs who are 2,000 or 3,000 years behind the Jews in civilization.*[92]

This February comment is echoed in a May 1918 letter from Chaim Weizmann in Tel Aviv-Jaffa to Balfour, complaining that English administrators of Palestine are ignoring the

> <u>*fundamental qualitative difference*</u> *between Jew and Arab....The present system tends on the contrary to level down the Jews to the status of a native, and in many cases the English Administrator follows the convenient rule of looking on the Jews as so many natives.*[93]

During April 7-10 1918 executive committee meeting, in a written submission, A. Leo Weil, noted the non-sectarian goals of the AJC, and worried that a Jewish state could oppress non-Jews:

> *To obtain for the Jews in every part of the world civil and religious rights; to protect them against unfavorable discrimination, and to secure for them equality of... opportunity... The purpose of this Committee was to obtain these rights, prevent this discrimination and secure these opportunities in and from respective Governments and communities in which the Jew, because he was in the minority, and of the prejudice against him, needed a spokesman and a defender.*
>
> *If a national home in Palestine be established, it may be that there too the good offices of this Committee may become necessary to protect a minority against an arrogant majority.*[94]

---

92 Page 649, *ibid.*
93 Chaim Weitzman to Arthur James Balfour, May 30, 1918, Tel Aviv-Jaffa, typewritten copy of letter on ZOA stationary, box 1, file 5, Papers of Louis Lipsky, P-672, AJHS. Emphasis added. Also available in PRO FO 371/3395.
94 April 7-10, 1918 meeting, MINUTES VOL. IV EXECUTIVE COMMITTEE Jan. 13, 1918 - May 27, 1923, page 679, AJC.

The AJC Statement: "A Weak Straddle"?

The statement on the British declaration was the beginning of AJC's support for "upbuilding" of a Jewish "national home" in Palestine, while abstaining from the Jewish nationalism gaining among the American Jews.

Prof. Jacob H. Hollander voted against the statement, calling it a "weak straddle":

> *The Zionistic propaganda has heretofore had the futility of a mirage; at this juncture it has the peril of a menace. At the very moment when Jewish patriotism and loyalty are challenged - none the less actually, because in inarticulate manner - at the moment when a ringing assertion of our organic integration with American citizenry and our unswerving devotion of its ideals - might be expected from us, we, the presumed spokesmen of American Jewry, are to content ourselves with a two-faced compromise that gives color to every charge of national parasitism and opportunist allegiance, directed against us.*[95]

In 1919, Marshall seemed to think the AJC statement had been definitive.

> *In April last the American Jewish Committee defined its position in terms <u>which could not be misunderstood</u>, which indicated that, while it hailed with satisfaction the Balfour Declaration, it did so because of the two conditions annexed, namely, that it would not affect the rights of the non-Jewish inhabitants of Palestine and that it was not to be regarded as in any way affecting the status of Jews who lived in other lands.*[96]

The "straddle" executed is well-illustrated in the highlighted paragraphs from the statement:

> *The American Jewish Committee was organized primarily to obtain for the Jews in every part of the world civil and religious rights, to protect them against*

---

95 April 7-10, 1918 meeting, MINUTES VOL. IV EXECUTIVE COMMITTEE Jan. 13, 1918 - May 27, 1923, page 680, AJC.
96 Louis Marshall to Simon Wolf March 4, 1919, *Louis Marshall, Champion of Liberty: Selected Papers and Addresses*, Jewish Publication Society, Philadelphia, 1957, vol. 1, pages 723-24. Emphasis added.

unfavorable discrimination, and to secure for them equality of economic, social, and educational opportunity. These will continue to be its objects.
The Committee regards it as axiomatic that the Jews of the United States have here established a permanent home for themselves and their children, have acquired the rights and assumed the correlative duties of American citizenship, and recognize their unqualified allegiance to this country, which they love and cherish, and of whose people they constitute an integral part.
<u>This Committee, however, is not unmindful that there are Jews everywhere who, moved by traditional sentiment, yearn for a home in the Holy Land for the Jewish people. This hope, nurtured for centuries, has our whole-hearted sympathy.</u>
<u>We recognize, however, that but a part of the Jewish people would take up their domicile in Palestine. The greater number will continue to live in the lands of whose citizenship they now form a component part, where they enjoy full civil and religious liberty, and where, as loyal and patriotic citizens, they will maintain and develop the principles and institutions of Judaism.</u>
When, therefore, the British Government recently made the declaration, now supported by the French Government, that "they view with favor the establishment in Palestine of a national home for the Jewish people, and will use their best endeavors to facilitate the achievement of this object," the announcement was received by this Committee with profound appreciation. The conditions annexed to this declaration are regarded as of essential importance, stipulating as they do that " nothing shall be done which may prejudice the civil and religious rights of existing non-Jewish communities in Palestine or the rights and political status enjoyed by Jews in any other country." These conditions correspond fully with the general purposes for which this Committee has striven and with the ideals of the Jews of America.
The opportunity will be welcomed by this Committee to aid in the realization of the British declaration, under such protectorate or suzerainty as the peace congress may determine, and, to that end, to co-operate with those who, attracted by religious or historic associations, shall

> *seek to establish in Palestine a centre for Judaism, for the stimulation of our faith, for the pursuit and development of literature, science, and art in a Jewish environment, and for the rehabilitation of the land.*[97]

---

[97] AJYB, Vol 20 (1918-19), pages 406-407.

"Upbuilding" Palestine—Forming the Jewish Agency

FEBRUARY 1924, Louis Marshall chaired a "Non-Partisan Conference to Consider Palestinian Problems" at the Hotel Astor. Co-conveners were Marshall, Cyrus Adler, Herbert H. Lehman, and Horace Stern.[98]

The conference was a step to create the Jewish Agency. The Jewish Agency was to take over from the Zionist Organization the League of Nations Mandate-assigned duties duties of implementing Jewish "upbuilding" (development) in Palestine.

In conference, Marshall spoke of the Jews of eastern Europe traumatized by oppression, the World War, and continuing strife, who wished to emigrate to Palestine, and stated Jews were obligated to take Britain's "great gift":

We cannot be indifferent to their wishes and to their hopes and to their desires. They are entitled to leave those lands and to seek homes elsewhere. Where shall they find them? Are we not too familiar with the sad fact that a policy is being formulated and is being urged, not only here but in other countries, which forbids immigration, which closes the doors of opportunity? ...And then, again, the British Government issued this Balfour Declaration--universally regarded as a Government which has always been the harbor of freedom and liberty and liberal ideas. France and Italy and other European Governments acquiesced in the adoption of that Declaration...England naturally expected that this great gift which it made, this great opportunity which it created, would be seized by the Jews and that for which they had called and that which had been granted to them, would be appreciated. It had the right to expect that the Jews would not hold themselves aloof....What would be said of the Jews of America, the richest community of Jews in the world, the

---

98 *Proceedings of Non-Partisan Conference to Consider Palestinian Problems*, 1924, 956:173 N, AJC Library. The conference was addressed by Louis Marshall, Dr. Chaim Weizmann, Dr. Arthur Ruppin, Judge Irving Lehman, David A. Brown, Dr. Abraham Simon, Judge Horace M. Stern, Dr. Leo K. Frankel, Col. Herbert H. Lehman, Samuel C. Lamport, Maurice Wertheim, Dr. Cyrus Adler, James Becker, Dr. Solomon Solis-Cohen, and Oscar Berman.

> most powerful and the most influential and the most
> happy, when at such a time as this, when they are called
> upon to perform, they smugly sit down, put their hands
> in their pockets...
> <u>I am afraid, I am afraid that non-action of that kind,
> indifference of that character, can do to us a thousand
> times more harm than all the Ku Klux Klans and Henry
> Fords that you could crowd into this great city.</u>⁹⁹

Chaim Weizmann presented his vision of a future harmonious Palestine:
> And I myself have repeatedly quoted Switzerland as one
> example. In Switzerland you have three civilizations
> living side by side and working for the common end of a
> beautiful Switzerland. I wish to God that there should be
> a Palestine in which three great religions and races could
> live side by side and work for the common end of a
> beautiful Palestine which has a word and a message to
> give to the world. And that is surely an aim which is
> worthy of anybody. (Applause.)¹⁰⁰

Judge Horace Stern likened querying the future of Jewish Palestine to cross-examining a child about what it will be when it grows up before giving it food.
> We will give the child the food, and if through our efforts
> it grows to manhood, we will let the future take care of
> itself, hoping that whether it be Zionist or non-Zionist, it
> will do the right thing at that time, under the guidance of
> God, and conditions which develop as time goes on and
> which human agencies can never foresee.¹⁰¹

Dr. Lee K. Frankel discussed the implications of American Jews instituting what might become a foreign government:
> If the future program of the Zionist Organization means
> a political state, then I think we are determining
> problems of principle, and they must be considered. ...I
> might as well be asked to join with a group in the United
> States who are intending to develop a monarchy in this
> country--a proposition absolutely foreign to my own
> conviction of a republican or democratic form of

---

99 Page 11-13, *ibid.*
100 Page 83, *ibid.*
101 Page 53, *ibid.*

> government.
> ...Is its immediate program, its program for the future, the program which presumably has been developed in the past, a program of the development of a political entity in Palestine supposedly run by the Jews?[102]

Chaim Weizmann told the conference:
> There is a saying that Palestine is destined to unite the Jews of the world. The first beginning of a tentative unity is being made in this resolution. Who will be the man who will raise his hand to stop the progress of unity. (Applause.)[103]

Meetings in New York were separate from the realities of "nation-building" spirit among the new Jewish Palestinians, for whom the caveats of limitation of the Balfour Declaration had little meaning:
> We'll build our land, our homeland
> We'll build our land, our homeland
> Because this land, this land is for us
> We'll build our land, our homeland
> It is our blood command, it is the generations' command
> We'll build our land despite our destroyers
> We'll build our land with our will-power.[104]

Dr. Solomon Solis-Cohen told the Palestine conference that he left Zionist Organization over the question of a Jewish State,
> as one who...went outside of the Zionist Organization upon the political question, because he believes that the Jews of America should be American in nationality, and the Jews of Britain, British in nationality, and the Jews everywhere loyal citizens of the governments under which they reside.
> Dr. Weizmann(interrupting): So do the Zionists.

---
102 Page 60, *ibid*.
103 Page 84, *ibid*.
104 "Nivne Artzenu," "We Will Build Our Land," Zionist song, 1928. Geography Professor Oren Yiftachel writes, "The Judaization program was premised on a hegemonic myth cultivated since the rise of Zionism, namely that 'the land' (*Haaretz*) belongs to the Jewish people, and only to the Jewish people. An exclusive form of settling ethno-nationalism developed in order quickly to 'indigenize' immigrant Jews, and to conceal, trivialize, or marginalize the Palestinian past." --'ETHNOCRACY': THE POLITICS OF JUDAIZING ISRAEL/PALESTINE, published in *Constellations*, 1999, Vol. 6, 364-391,
http://www.geog.bgu.ac.il/members/yiftachel/new_papers_eng/Constellations-print.htm

> Dr. Solis-Cohen (resuming): But that being the position, I am speaking as one outside of the Zionist Organization in saying that I believe non-Zionists dare not shut their ears to this voice which says, "Come and help us build up the Holy Land; come and help us to make it a land of safety for our brethren; come and help us make it a beacon light to all the world, a beacon light of civilization, of truth, of faith, of humanity."[105]

The AJC was informed clearly of the Arab refusal to cooperate with the British/Zionist plan:

> ...in Palestine itself, the attempt to buy off the Arab irreconcilables having culminated in the offer of an Arab Agency and its rejection, the [UK] Government seems to have made up its mind that, if the co-operation of the Arab malcontents cannot be secured, the Administration must in future be carried on without it.
> ...In the 1923 [British] Election Palestine was hardly mentioned, either in the Press or on the platform. One or two bodies...made attempts to bring before the electorate the alleged grievances of the Palestine Arabs, but the electorate declined to show the smallest interest in the subject.
> ...every effort to secure Arab co-operation having failed, nothing remained but to carry on the Administration of Palestine without it.[106]

In May 1924, a meeting followed for the initial establishment of the Jewish Agency, hosted in Louis Marshall's home. Cyrus Adler, Chaim Weizmann and Louis Lipsky were among those present.[107]

A minimum of American Jewish representation in the Jewish Agency was specified.[108] This had no relation to an anticipated proportion of American Jewish *chalutzim* (pioneers) emigrating to the *Yishuv*, but

---

[105] *Palestine Non-Partisan Conference*, Page 75-76.
[106] Zionist Organization, "REPORT ON THE POLITICAL SITUATION FEBRUARY 1924," box 4, file "Zionist-Non-Zionist Relations 1923-1926/Jewish Agency, Marshall-Weizmann," Marshall Correspondence Subject Files, AJC.
[107] "Minutes of the Meeting on the Jewish Agency," May 4, 1924, *ibid*. It should be noted that this pre-dates by five years what is the conventional recorded date of the founding of the Jewish Agency.
[108] "...an agency to consist of a council of 150 members and an executive committee of 18, to be selected by the council, of whom 50% will represent the Zionists and 50% the non-Zionists, and of the non-Zionists 40% should be apportioned to the United States of America and the remainder to the other countries of the world..." *Ibid*.

rather reflected the financial and organizational resources of Zionism in the prosperous and free Jews of America.

> *On the material side, the debt of Palestine and the whole Jewish people during the years of war to American Jewry is incalculable. When the United States was neutral, and the American Jews had access to the East, they promptly assumed the responsibility which had fallen upon them. If the centre of gravity of the commonwealth of Jewry has passed from Russia to the United States, that is due, not simply to wealth and numerical strength, but to the fact that, when the call came, American Jews answered it.*[109]

The concept of a Jewish Agency to include both Zionist and non-Zionist leadership was difficult and episodic in execution. (In 1943, Joseph Proskauer told the AJC annual meeting, "It was supposed to be composed of an equal number of Zionists and anti-Zionists. It was not supposed to be a Zionist body, and as always happens when a negative group is wedded to a positive group, the positive group ate up the negative group, and to all intents and purposes, the Jewish Agency became a pro-Zionist activity."[110] [111])

Rabbi Elmer Berger wrote that Weizmann was executing a Zionist Organization plan of misdirection,

> *for enlisting the support and participation of the leadership of essentially anti-Zionist American Jews. To bridge the gap Weizmann coined the term "non-Zionist". The nomenclature was intended to identify a Jew who was willing to contribute material aid to the building of the "national home" but was recognized as opposing the concept of "Jewish" nationalism....*
>
> *The principle focus of Weizmann's "diplomacy" were the leaders of the American Jewish Committee, in the mid-1920's the most prestigious collection of American Jews, generous philanthropists, but anti-Zionist almost*

---

[109] H. Sacher, "A Jewish Palestine," *Atlantic*, June 1919, page 121.

[110] Address of Joseph M. Proskauer, AJC Thirty-Sixth Annual Report, 1943, Page 48. Also American Jewish Yearbook, Vol. 45, page 643.

[111] Louis Marshall wrote on the Zionists' advantage of having a positive platform, in a letter to Max Senor, September 26, 1918: "The Zionists, whether their views be sound or otherwise, are the advocates of an affirmative policy. It is one that appeals to the imagination. It is replete with poetry." *Correspondence on the Advisability of Calling a Conference For the Purpose of Combating Zionism*, Zionist Organization of America, 1918. *ZP-*PZX n.c. 2, no. 19 [Microfilm], NYPL Dorot Jewish Collection, pages 10-11.

to a man. How this mesalliance was finally consummated is a story of naivete on the part of American Jews. They believed Weizmann's tactically watered-down version of Zionist aspirations and relied upon the Mandatory to enforce the "safeguard" clauses of the Balfour Declaration, protecting <u>both</u> Palestinian Arabs and anti-Zionist Jews from any possible threats to their existing nationality status by any unrestricted Zionist aggressiveness.[112]

---

[112] Rabbi Elmer Berger, *The structure of the Zionist movement in the United States*, Paper No. 10, International Organisation for the Elimination of All Forms of Racial Discrimination (EAFORD), 1983, page 3. See discussion of Weizmann's plans for "reshuffling" populations, page 109.

SEPTEMBER 26, 1891.

Israel, the Source of Modern Ideals.

"Idealists, dreamers, fanatics, perchance at times anarchists, the children of Israel were nevertheless the first people to recognize the necessity of an amalgamation of the human and the divine. Israel had a genius for popular idealism. The basis of the Hebrew constitution is altruism. The kernel of the laws lays more stress upon the human than the divine. Of the Ten Commandments six command us to deal justly by others. A keen appreciation of the rights of the weaker classes is the special feature of the legislation of Israel, which distinguishes it from the legislation of other nations.

"Modern economists are merely rendering the ideals of Israel intelligible to the present age. It is becoming more patent daily that Israel is the source of modern ideals."—*Professor Lyman P. Powell, of Johns Hopkins University, in American Hebrew.*

This New York Herald article illustrates the now-obsolescent use of the name "Israel" to denote the Jewish people as a group. (Lucien Moss scrapbook collection, P-14, box 2, volume 3, AJHS.)

Interpreting Balfour

The British declaration was ambiguous in what a Jewish "national home" in Palestine meant, and the Zionist Organization personalities displayed similar ambiguity. In 1918, the Advisory Committee of the Zionist Organization wrote to Major Lionel de Rothschild of the League of British Jews, "No claim is made or will be made that Jews constitute a separate political nationality all over the world," and that "neither in the present or the future should there be any discrimination among the inhabitants of Palestine with respect to citizenship or civil rights."[113]

The League extracted these pledges, in exchange for its approval of the Declaration, from Herbert Samuel, writing for the Advisory Committee, which included Weizmann and Sokolow. The pledges seem to embody the future incongruous match of both sectarian entitlement and equality:

> *If a "National Home" is to be established for the Jews in Palestine, in accordance with the Government declaration, the growth of the Jewish population must be fostered. This can best be accomplished by securing, at the outset, a right of pre-emption with respect to certain lands, and by other economic means. The agency for carrying these measures into effect should be specifically Jewish organization, which should be independent of the Government of the Country. Zionists hold that, neither in the present nor in the future, should there be any discrimination in Palestine with respect to citizenship or civil rights, on the ground of race or of religion, among the inhabitants of the country; any such discrimination would be in direct contradiction of the principles of religious equality for which Jews have contended throughout the world for centuries.*[114]

In detailed exchanges of letters with Louis Marshall, de Rothschild, of the League of British Jews, "An Association of British Subjects Professing the Jewish Religion," approved of the AJC statement on the British (Balfour) declaration, "except that we object on principle to the phrase 'a National home for the Jewish people.'"

---

113 Lionel de Rothschild to D. Lloyd George(PM), 18 December 1918, file "Palestine/League of British Jews 1918-19," General Correspondence 1906-1932, box 16, AJC.
114 Herbert Samuel to Waley Cohen, November 2, 1918, *ibid.*

> The League cordially sympathises with the desire to make Palestine a centre for Judaism, for the stimulation of our faith and for the advancement of Jewish literature and learning. The League is in cordial agreement with the desire for the rehabilitation of the land.[115]

Marshall wrote for the AJC:
> The phrases which you have criticized are naturally those that would, as one might have expected, give rise to controversy. Indeed their adoption followed prolonged discussion and debate. When read in its entirety, however it was our opinion that our Statement does not in any way commit us to Jewish Nationalism in the political as distinguished from the ethnical sense of the term. We sought to make it entirely clear that we recognized no political allegiance whatsoever, save that flowing from our American citizenship, and that whilst we could and do sympathize with and are willing to aid those who wish <u>a</u> home in Palestine, we do not look upon such a home as <u>the</u> home of the Jewish people, regarding them as a unit. Unquestionably there are Jews in every land who have for centuries yearned for such a home, and many still eagerly desire it. The realization of this pious wish unquestionably would be hailed with satisfaction by every true Jew who loves the traditions of his faith. You will note that we have carefully refrained from accepting the phrase "<u>the homeland of the Jewish people</u>," which has latterly sprung into vogue. Not even Herzl used it. To my mind it is an historical and a practical absurdity. The objection to the words "a <u>National</u> Home for <u>the</u> Jewish People," is from your point of view entirely natural. Let me, however, call your attention to the fact that we do not in our Statement use capitals, as you do in your quotation, and that <u>a</u> home is mentioned and not <u>the</u> home for the Jewish people. Nor is the phrase ours. It is that of the British Declaration. We merely state as a fact that we greeted the announcement made by your Government "with profound appreciation" and that we shall welcome the opportunity to aid in the realization of the British Declaration, <u>under such protectorate or suzerainty as the Peace Congress may determine</u> "and to that end to co-

---

[115] de Rothschild to Marshall, June 19, 1918, *ibid*.

operate" <u>for certain specific purposes, which do not include the establishment of an independent Jewish State or Commonwealth.</u> I may add that before our committee adopted its Statement, I submitted the draft to Mr. Lansing, our Secretary of State, for his criticism and comments, and received his approval.*

We deemed it our duty for many reasons, both practical and sentimental, to give expression to our attitude toward the British Declaration, but at the same time considered it highly important to give emphasis to those controlling principles which we look upon as essential to the preservation of our status as American citizens, and to file a caveat against future misinterpretation of the theory on which our acceptance of the Declaration is based. It was also our firm conviction that it might prove unfortunate if at this juncture we should say or do anything that might be regarded be regarded by your Government or by ours as lacking in appreciation of the exalted statesmanship and the humane motives underlying the Declaration, or that might be interpreted by our enemies as hostile to the policies of Great Britain and those of here allies who have endorsed the Declaration.[116]

---

* The AJC was consistently concerned not to inadvertently counter US policy. In other matters, such as immigration or proposed legislation, they relied on top-level relationships allowing them to confer with leadership in government.

116 Marshall to de Rothschild, July 12, 1918, *ibid.*

"Zionism is but an incidence of a far-reaching plan."

Following the British Declaration and the swelling American Jewish interest in Palestine, the Rev. Dr. (Rabbi) David Philipson circulated a letter asking:
> *Is Zionism all of Judaism? Shall the Zionistic party be the spokesman for American Jewry?*[117]

In 1918, in the World War, the AJC encountered the idea that Zionism is US policy, and that opposition to Zionism was opposition to US policy.

AJC President Louis Marshall lays out this imperative, with a chilling warning, in a Sept. 28, 1918 letter to Max Senor, reproduced in a Zionist Organization of America booklet of letters to counter Rabbi Philipson's call for an anti-Zionist conference:

> *Subsequent to the time when Dr. Philipson wrote his letter, President Wilson expressed his personal views in support of the principles laid down in the Balfour Declaration. France, Italy and Greece have formally adopted the terms of the Declaration. There is, therefore, a unanimity in sentiment on the part of the Allied Powers, which makes the Balfour Declaration a part of their united position.*
>
> *The American Jewish Committee, although its members in the main are non-Zionists, recognized the political importance of the Declaration, and its strategic significance as a factor in the effort to defeat the Central Powers and for strengthening the cause of the Entente. ...*
>
> *I am confident that the Balfour Declaration and its acceptance by the other Powers, is an act of the highest diplomacy. <u>It means both more and less than appears on the surface. Zionism is but an incidence of a far-reaching plan. It is merely a convenient peg on which to hang a powerful weapon. All the protests that non-Zionists may make would be futile to affect that policy.</u>*
>
> *It that were the sole consequence of a protest, I would stand mute, but I am confident that action in hostility to the carefully formulated pronouncements of the Allied Governments would be resented, the Jews as a whole would be the sufferers, and those engaged in combating*

---
117 American Jewish Committee Minutes, Vol. IV, Executive Committee, Jan. 13, 1918 - May 27, 1923, page 729, AJC..

> *what those Governments would regard as their policy would place themselves in serious jeopardy.* <u>*It would subject them individually to hateful and obnoxious investigation. It would put them under suspicion. I could give concrete examples of a most impressive nature in support of what I have said.*</u>[118]

The message is the same in a Sept. 3, 1918 letter from Marshall to Rabbi Philipson:

> *"To combat Zionism at this time is to combat the Governments of England, France and Italy, and to some extent our Government in so far as its political interests are united with those of the nations which it has joined in fighting the curse of autocracy."*[119]

Jacob H. Schiff illustrated the fear of schism among Jews which hobbled active opposition to Zionism(Sept. 5, 1918):

> *Your proposition[for a Jewish conference against Zionism], in the nature of things as they have developed, cannot be successful and will only bring forth bitterness, recrimination, and marked division among the Jewish People of this country, which, I am sure, is greatly to be deprecated.*[120]

Oscar Straus emphasized a "Reasons of State" argument, regarding relations of the Jews to the Powers(Sept. 3, 1918):

> *In view of the fact that Great Britain, France and other allied nations through their highest officials, have given assurances of the welfare of the Jews in Palestine, regardless of the fact whether one is a Zionist or not, to oppose such a beneficent purpose on the part of a section of our people can only be hurtful and show not only a lack of unanimity, but of appreciation for those welcome assurances, which should receive not only the gratitude not only of Jews as such, but as Americans, for this first significant and concrete move on the part of the allied nations to assure freedom of development for subject nationalities.*[121]

---

118 *Correspondence on the Advisability of Calling a Conference for the Purpose of Combating Zionism*, Zionist Organization of America, New York City, 1918. Page. 8. NY Public Library, *ZP-*PZX n.c. 2, no. 19 [Microfilm] Emphasis added.
119 Page 7, *ibid.*
120 Page 6, *ibid.*
121 Page 4, *ibid.*

"We need work of a patient, simple kind."

New Zionist leader Louis D. Brandeis had been repeatedly promoting a different, but complementary, angle:

> There is no inconsistency between loyalty to America and loyalty to Jewry. The Jewish spirit, the product of our religion and experiences, is essentially modern and essentially American. Not since the destruction of the Temple have the Jews in spirit and in ideals been so fully in harmony with the noblest aspirations of the country in which they lived....
> Indeed, loyalty to America demands rather that each American Jew become a Zionist. For only through the ennobling effect of its strivings can we develop the best that is in us and give to this country the full benefit of our great inheritance.[122]
>
> ....
> Your loyalty to America, your loyalty to Judaism, should lead you to support the Zionist cause.[123]

In a theme that recurs in discussions of Zionism, Churchill in 1920 said,

> "The struggle between the Zionist and Bolshevik Jews is little less than a struggle for the soul of the Jewish people. In this case, redeeming the land is saving the Jews for the good of the nations.[124]

The American Communist writer Albert Weisbord demonstrates two common lines of discussion about "the Jew," the "unnaturalness" of their

---

[122] Louis D. Brandeis, "The Jewish Problem: How To Solve It," Speech to the Conference of Eastern Council of Reform Rabbis, April 25, 1915,
www.law.louisville.edu/library/collections/brandeis/node/234

[123] Louis D. Brandeis, *Zionism and Patriotism*, Federation of American Zionists, New York, N.Y., 1915,
http://cojs.org/fullrez/zionist_movement/Zionism_and_Patriotism.pdf

[124] *Illustrated Sunday Herald*, Feb. 8. 1920. Quoted in *Bolsheviks and British Jews: the Anglo-Jewish Community, Britain, and the Russian Revolution*, by Sharman Kadish, Routledge, 1992, page 138. Chaim Weizmann and others "were not averse to exploiting exaggerated Foreign Office fears about the Jewish role in Bolshevism in order to secure British support for a Jewish Palestine." Martin Gilbert, in his *Churchilll and the Jews*, Henry Holt, 2007, page 28, says "The Fact that the Zionist Jews had been prepared to try to prevent the Bolsheviks coming to power and pulling Russia out of the war, meant much to him. He saw the dangerous situation to Britain, France and the United States on the Western Front in March 1918, that resulted both from Russia's withdrawal from the war, and from the growing tyranny of Bolshevism inside Russia."

character, and their use to larger forces:
> For close to 2,000 years the majority of the Jews have been divorced from the land. The wholesome communion and nature that agricultural production implies has been lost to them. All- rounded development cannot be theirs. They lack a certain robustness, a healthy relation to nature that should be the heritage of all peoples.[125]
>
> To become a Zionist means for the Jew again to become a nationalist and to push himself back 2000 years. It means to try to build up a capitalist state at the very moment when capitalism is doomed to perish and the state to wither away. It means to become the dupes and the tools of this or that imperialism and to be used as a club to crush the colonial peoples of the near and far east....On the other hand, as soon as it is convenient for the ruling powers, the Jew will be made the scape-goat and sacrificed first of all.[126]

This curiosity, from 1916, gives a good example of the "return to the land and re-make the Jew," redemption-through-agricultural-labor ideology of Zionism:

> "We need work of a patient, simple kind," said Meir. "Day in, day out, the months and years that I have planned this little garden have been one [of] patient labor; nothing complex or subtle; everything depending on sheer honesty at every stage. We Jews have to commence life again, to leave the artificial fictitious world of abstractions. The return to agriculture will be the redemption of our race. What is Judaism? It is the simple, practical, true-hearted life of the Bible as set forth in the Bible, becoming a mighty power for us. Here I find Judaism. Here my soul was bred, the soul of my race. What a sense of peace has come to me!"[127]

An article in The Atlantic expanded this line of Zionism,
> It is Jewish self-consciousness that speaks through Zionism: 'At present we are not, as a people, farmers, mechanics, soldiers, engineers, statesmen, sportsmen.

---

[125] Albert Weisbord, "The Jew, Capitalism and Communism," Part I, *Class Struggle*, Vol. 2, No. 1, Jan. 1935, http://www.weisbord.org/FiveOne.htm

[126] *Ibid*, Part 2, Vol. 2, No. 5, Feb. 1935, http://www.weisbord.org/FiveTwo.htm

[127] Nahum Sokolow, "The New Jew" in *Zionism and the Jewish Future* by Various Writers. Edited by H. Sacher. Introduction by C. Weizmann. John Murray, London. 1916, page 226. "Meir," the subject of the story has settled in Palestine in the Upper Galilee, married a daughter of a Petach Tikvah settler, and had two children.

We have been obliged by our anomalous situation as permanent strangers to specialize in a few directions. Henceforth we shall be everything, develop every human aptitude and power in our own measure, and so meet the calumny that we are in our souls part-men, cunning and parasitic. On the soil of our fathers we shall become what we are, renew our cultural fertility, and repay mankind blessing for persecution.' This is a programme whose conception compels admiration. Further, its significance is unique: there are no near parallels in law or in history. [128]

Complementary to this is the pointed comment from G.K. Chesterton, a good example of anti-Semitic Zionism:

It is our whole complaint against the Jew that he does not till the soil or toil with the spade... He must be washed in mud, that he may be clean.

Chesterton expresses the concern that too few Jews will leave England, as he would prefer not too many remain to his taste:

It might be worth while for England to take risks to settle the Jewish problem; but not to take risks merely to unsettle the Arab problem, and leave the Jewish problem unsolved.[129]

In 1916, English Zionist Paul Goodman said a purpose of Zionism was to counter the loss of identity of emancipated Jews, as much as provide safety for oppressed Jews:

The effects of emancipation are, from the Jewish point of view, negative...In the memorable declaration of Herzl at the opening of the first Congress, Zionism was to be a return of the Jews to the Jewish people, even before their return to the Jewish land.[130]

At the time of the Balfour declaration, British cabinet member Edwin S. Montagu identified it as "anti-Semitic in result."

I claim that the lives that British Jews have led, that the aims that they have had before them, that the part that they have

---

[128] William Earnest Hocking, "Palestine: An Impasse?" The Atlantic, June 1930, http://www.theatlantic.com/magazine/archive/1969/12/palestine-an-impasse/6750/

[129] G.K. Chesterton, *The New Jerusalem*, George H. Doran Company, 1921. Pages 298, 299, vi.

[130] Paul Goodman, "The Spirit of Zionism" in *Zionism: Problems and Views*, Paul Goodman and Arthur D. Lewis, eds., introduction by Max Nordau, Fisher Unwin, London, 1916, page 270.

> *played in our public life and our public institutions, have entitled them to be regarded, not as British Jews, but as Jewish Britons. ...I would ask of a British Government sufficient tolerance to refuse a conclusion which makes aliens and foreigners by implication, if not at once by law, of all their Jewish fellow-citizens.* [131]

While chairman of *aliyah* promotion organization *Nefesh b'Nefesh*, former Israeli ambassador to the United States Daniel Ayalon solicited funds from an evangelical American Christian congregation for emigration of Jewish US citizens to Israel, to "ensure that Israel will always stay Jewish demographically... bringing Jews from the west namely the United States, Canada, and some from the UK, will be the answer. Also, if you look from a practical point of view, this is the only place now, the only reservoir of Jews outside of Israel are basically in the West."[132]

Montagu's fears have been borne out, in that building of a Jewish state has meant destruction of Jewish communities around the world, in addition to dislodging the Arab community of Palestine.

Israeli symbiosis with American Christian conservatives who regard the United States as a "Christian" country has paid foreign policy dividends for the State of Israel — at the price of casting Jewish Americans as nascent Israelis. In November 2009, former Republican vice-presidential candidate Sarah Palin said the "population of Israel is, is going to grow. More and more Jewish people will be flocking to Israel in the days and weeks and months ahead. And I don't think that the Obama administration has any right to tell Israel that the Jewish settlements cannot expand."[133]

In 2006, Pastor James Hagee and other Christian Zionists founded Christians United for Israel (CUFI), now claimed to be "the largest pro-Israel organization in the United States." CUFI is significant in Washington lobbying for the State of Israel.[134]

---

[131] http://www.jewishvirtuallibrary.org/jsource/History/Montagumemo.html
[132] "Israeli Ambassador Daniel Ayalon Visit," video recording of visit at Cedar Park Christian Church, Bothell, State of Washington, USA, December 2, 2007, to raise funds for *Nefesh b'Nefesh*, at 1:07,
http://www.tvw.org/media/mediaplayer.cfm?evid=2007120062&TYPE=V&bhcp=1
[133] http://www.csmonitor.com/World/Global-News/2009/1118/sarah-palin-urges-israel-settlement-expansion-attacks-barack-obama
[134] http://www.cufi.org/site/PageServer?pagename=about_AboutCUFI

"The American blow will be more painful."

Though leadership of American Zionism by native-born men like Louis D. Brandeis would exist, the bulk of Zionist interest in a Jewish home resided in those American Jews who were less acclimated and less sure of their place in America. A survey of "Pre-Herzlian Zionism In America As Reflected In The Yiddish Press" says expulsion from America was near to mind in that population.
> This possibility was discussed dispassionately and without bitterness almost, as if it were a logical proposition and the inevitable fate of diaspora existence.

A poem found by the survey author supposed:
> In America preparations are made to give you a kick
> A blow or a tickle with a knife
> You found Ivan's blow painful
> The American blow will be more painful.[135]

At the same time, estrangement from religion in American society was anticipated — "the haunting fear that America, in spite of its permissive atmosphere, means the religious alienation of our children."[136]

A survey of Yiddish-language newspapers in NY in the 1925 found, "Aside from the [Labor/Socialist] *Vorwaerts*, all of the present newspapers are decidedly Zionistic."[137]

---

[135] Shlomo Noble, "Pre-Herzlian Zionism In America As Reflected In The Yiddish Press" in *Early Zionist History in America*, American Jewish Historical Society, New York, 1958, page 44.
[136] Page 43, *ibid*.
[137] "The Yiddish Press—An Americanizing Agency," by Mordecai Soltes, Ph.D., AJYB, Vol. 26 (1924-25), page 70.

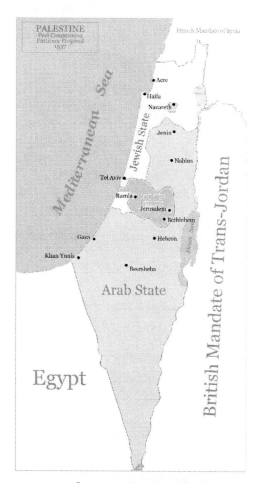

1937 Peel Commission Plan of Partition, rejected by the Arab side. The Jewish side was equivocal. Militant Zionism claimed Palestine and Trans-Jordan for a Jewish State. In the plan, the British maintained Mandate for a core area of Jerusalem with a "corridor" to the coast, and a large number of Arabs would have been "transferred" from the Jewish state. (Map by Yan Nasonov.)

II. The AJC until Palestine Partition

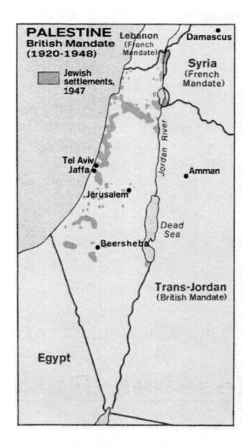

Jewish-settled areas in Palestine at time of 1947 Partition vote; map produced by the U.S. Central Intelligence Agency. (http://www.lib.utexas.edu/maps/historical/israel_hist_1973.jpg) See areas assigned to Jews and Arabs in the UN Partition Plan, page 140.

> *There seems to be a madness that seizes all people who touch the Palestine problem directly.*
>
> Joseph Proskauer (1947)[138]

"Beyond any consideration of good or evil."

Blaustein's — **and** the American Jewish Committee's — perspective on Palestine and the Jews was a particularly American one.

The AJC's counsel to the Roosevelt and Truman administrations had been distinctly anti-Zionist while advocating for open Jewish immigration to Palestine.

Proskauer wrote President Truman "certain salient points" June 6, 1945 :

> *(1) We emphasize the importance of measures for Protection of Human Rights; abrogation of racial legislation; indemnification; repatriation; migration problems; statelessness; and war crimes. We do not concentrate on the Palestinian question.*
> *(2) <u>We distinguish sharply between the importance of Palestine as a place of homeland and refuge and the question of statehood for Palestine.</u>*
> *(3) We have contended that it was ill-advised to agitate for Jewish statehood under existing conditions. I deem it right in this connection to say to you that, in a conference*

---

[138] May 11, 1947 executive committee transcript, page 36, AJC. Compare with this quote about Jacob de Hass, "A blind spot of madness seems to form in the outlook of everyone who succumbs to the Zionist germ," Walid Khalidi, *From Haven to Conquest,* Institute for Palestine Studies, Beirut, 1971, page 185. Rabbi Abba Hillel Silver depicts Herzl as transformed "into the captive slave of an all-claiming, all-demanding, all-consuming ideal." Silver, *A Word in Its Season,* World Publishing, New York, 1972, page 407.

> *with Mr Blaustein shortly before he left Washington for the last time, President Roosevelt stated to us that he had come to this belief and that he saw in the extreme Zionist agitation grave danger for the world and for Palestine itself. He added his belief that Great Britain could not presently consider Jewish statehood. I write you this solely for your own information, as we have not deemed it proper to give publicity to this statement of President Roosevelt.*
>
> *(4) Accordingly, we stress at this time as the main objective for Palestine the modification of the British White Paper and the liberalization of Jewish immigration into Palestine, for that may become necessary for the relief of many thousand stricken European Jews.*
>
> *Through the introduction of the Department of State, we have urged this course on Lord Halifax...If this could be attained, we believe that it would satisfy the wishes of many thousands of those associated with the Zionist organizations, though, of course, not those of their members holding most extreme views.*
>
> ...
>
> *(6) In formulating our views we have endeavored to make every recommendation consistent with the primary objective of "aiding in the establishment of a world order that is just to every human being, irrespective of race, creed, or nationality".*[139]

The AJC were conscious of the presence and importance of the Arab population of Palestine, and reluctantly favored a plan for partition in 1946 to allow a Jewish-majority area, but with a distinctly American goal, as Blaustein says in his Baltimore speech:

> *...the Jewish section, when thought of in terms of a Jewish state, will be a Jewish state only in the sense that the United States, with a preponderance of Christian population, might be termed a Christian state.*

In September 1946 Proskauer reported to the Executive Board that he and Blaustein, for the AJC, had agreed to support the Jewish Agency in exchange for the Agency's retreat from insistence on all of Palestine for a

---

[139] Box 1.30, folder 416 "AJC - Truman, President," JHU. Quote Proskauer cites is from *To The Counselors of Peace*, American Jewish Committee, New York, 1945. Page 2. Emphasis added.

Jewish State — rather partition of Palestine into two states, one with a Jewish majority and control of immigration.[140]

This support for partition was premised on the fact that continuing international governance of Palestine, in the form of UN trusteeship — the AJC's first choice — was not viable.

> *Partition formally remained relatively low in the order of desirability. This situation is reflected in the AJC statement of May 1947 to UNSCOP. It will be remembered that partition was there advocated only if UNSCOP should find a declaration of prompt independence necessary; but the AJC felt that international trusteeship for a number of years would be preferable....Despite this lack of enthusiasm, the subsequent vigorous AJC effort to obtain United States support for UN adoption of partition was entirely logical....prompt Palestinian independence created a situation in which only two alternatives retained real significance: partition, and Arab domination.*[141]

Proskauer emphasized that it would be a Jewish majority state but a "so-called" Jewish state, and that he had insisted the Jewish Agency to add the words "so-called" and "only" in the following paragraph in their agreement:

> *The <u>so-called</u> Jewish State is not to be called by that name but will bear some appropriate geographical designation. It will be Jewish <u>only</u> in the sense that the Jews will form a majority of the population.*[142]

Proskauer told the executive committee that in the plan presented by Nahum Goldmann of the Agency to Proskauer,

> *All responsibility in regard to Palestine will henceforward devolve on the Jews of Palestine with the Jews in America maintaining merely a moral and spiritual concern in the new venture, but in no way*

---

140 "Address of Hon. Joseph M. Proskauer before the Executive Committee of the American Jewish Committee, Sunday, September 15, 1946," Executive Committee Transcript "Part 2," Archive box "Executive Committee Transcripts Oct. 1943-May 1947," AJC.

141 Milton Himmelfarb, "AJC Position on the Jewish State," Dec. 31, 1947, confidential memo, page 3, in binder "The Record of the American Jewish Committee in RE Palestine," Vol. 3, AJC.

142 Proskauer, Sept. 15, 1946 transcript *op. cit.*, page 11, repeated on page 21, AJC, emphasis in original.

> politically tied up with it.[143]
> ...A great obstacle has always been the intransigent Chauvinism of the Jewish Agency...[144]
> Mr Blaustein, I think I may say, and I, came to a general accord on the diplomatic handling of this very delicate and difficult situation. It was not helped by statements from agencies that the Jews are not (sic) a homeless people. I do not need to tell anybody here within the sound of my voice how thoroughly I have repudiated the idea of Jews being a homeless people in the sense of building up nationalism. I do not -- and I say this with all kindliness and without bitterness and without criticism of anybody -- think that it was helpful when Jews were trying to negotiate homes for these homeless Jews in those concentration camps to go abroad arguing an ideology out of all relationship, as I saw it as a negotiator, to the specific problem with which we were concerned....This is a side issue, that this moderate plan of the Agency encountered the bitterest opposition from the extremists like Dr. Silver.[145]

The debates in the executive committee as the AJC agreed to join in the push for Partition at the UN and with the US government, centered on ensuring that what they were endorsing would be congruent with the American lesson of a multitude of "nationalities" making a nation.

> Maurice B. Hexter: As some of you know who attended the meeting that Dr. Magnes addressed when he first came here, I deem it a source of the greatest possible danger to all Jewry and to the world that we face in Palestine a situation such as we face in all authoritarian countries that your youth has been bred in an atmosphere which endangers the peace of the countries in which they live as do the Comosols and a few years back the Italian Avantgardistas and the counterpart in Germany.
> And there is no task that faces Jewry more holy and more consequential in my opinion than to address ourselves to its detoxination(sic). Judge Proskauer referred to the intransigent nationalism. It was that, sir, and nothing else which drove me away from Palestine,

---
143 Page 12, *ibid*.
144 Page 15, *ibid*.
145 Page 21-22, *ibid*.

> *because I did not wish my daughter brought up in the atmosphere and the tempo of the marching streets because the streets re-echoed, as they did in Germany and as they did in Italy, to the tempo of youth raised on a diet which they could illy digest....*[146]

Their difference with nationalism is illustrated in an AJC memo of Jan. 13, 1948, where "the prevailing and dangerous predominance of unthinking emotionalism" is attributed to "the magic influence of the political witch-doctor." The difference of the AJC from political Zionists was stark:

> *Whether these extreme Zionists realize it or not, the fact remains that behind their mentality and program there is no less monstrosity than the idol of the State as an absolute totalitarian substance in itself, the State which is complete master not only over its own immediate subjects but also over every living Jewish body and soul the world over, beyond any consideration of good or evil.* [147]

The AJC recognized the ethnic warfare that was developing in Palestine:

> *Today there is genocidal strife going on in Palestine which has undermined the security of the entire Yishuv. While the Arabs are clearly the aggressors, the Jews are retaliating in kind, and the result is a war of mutual extermination on racial grounds, without mercy to young and old, women and babes. It is clear that the American Jewish Committee must do its utmost for contributing to the localization and quenching of the blaze, through all means of influence at its disposal, not only to avert the prevailing physical danger which may turn uncontrollable after the cessation of the Mandate, but also the moral and political repercussions which may deeply affect both the Jewish position outside Palestine, and the character of the Jewish state in Palestine. The present atmosphere of Palestine is a hotbed of ultra-nationalism and militarism out of which no democratic and humanitarians State may arise.*
> *Related to this latter situation is the endangered*

---

[146] Sept 15, 1946 executive committee meeting transcript, page 15, AJC.
[147] "Political Problems involved in the Palestine Solution," Jan. 13, 1948, page 3, in binder "Record of the American Jewish Committee in RE Palestine," Vol. 4, AJC.

> condition of the Jewish communities in the Arab
> countries. The American Jewish Committee has made it
> its business to intervene for the protection of these
> minorities, and must try to make this protection more
> effective than it is today in the face of a growing threat of
> massacres.[148]

The memo recognized the heroic image of the Zionist "nation-builder" that was emerging:

> ....We will have to attack, through many media reaching
> the average Jewish public, the childish and dangerous
> habit of personifying abstractions like the anti-Semites
> do, and making the so-called "Jewishness" of the
> otherwise over-assimilated and well-nigh nazified hyper-
> Zionist adventurer type an idol of worship and blind
> obedience.[149]

Illustratively, the American Jewish Committee wished to seem influential in the situation that was spinning out of its control:

> ...[In discussion of things to request from US
> administration:] *It would signally strengthen the political
> and educational authority*[of the AJC] *if all American
> official contributions to Palestine would result from our
> interventions, and could be announced by us. As the
> leading and recognized American Jewish organization,
> we are entitled to this consideration, and if we ask for it,
> we may obtain it.*[150]

The dire and colorful 22-page memo concludes that the AJC and Jewish Agency must adapt, "an adaptation without which a dangerous rift between the two wings of Jewish political creed and conviction would become inevitable."[151]

The "dangerous rift" must not imperil Jewish unity.

In a late 1945 memo[152] listing executive committee members who should not be proposed for re-election in the February 1946 annual meeting, three members were cited for involvement in the anti-Zionist

---
148 Page 4, *ibid.*
149 Page 15, *ibid.*
150 Page 14, *ibid.*
151 Page 22, *ibid.*
152 "Executive Committee Membership, October 17, 1945," unsigned typewritten document, box 1.26, file 372 "AJC Nominations, Elections, etc.," JHU.

American Council for Judaism. One, long-time member Leo M. Brown of Mobile, Alabama, was cited as an "extreme Zionist." (The reason most commonly cited was "doesn't attend meetings" or does not assist their local chapter. This category included Louis B. Mayer, of Culver City, California.)

AJC social science researcher Max Horkheimer[153] sent to John Slawson his 1945 misgivings about the consequences imminent from the "fallacies of Zionism," but ending with what seem the characteristic hopes for creating a concord among Jews (what Maurice Hexter called "this miasma of Jewish unity"):

> Sometime ago I had a conversation with Dr. Maurice Karpf.[154] As you know, he is one of the few non-Zionist members of the Jewish Agency for Palestine. As such he is taking a close interest in the political developments. His general outlook for the near future is rather dark. In particular, he is afraid Zionist policies within and without Palestine might lead to an acute situation, possibly to rioting and bloodshed. Only a strong assertion of the non-Zionist Jewish friends of Palestine can, in his opinion, prevent Judaism, as a whole, being held morally responsible for the fallacies of Zionism. Any delicate diplomatic situation which might arise for our own government in this connection will not fail to have repercussions on American Jewry. Since apart from the shortsighted and completely insignificant utterances of the [American] *Council for Judaism* no Jewish voice is heard in this country but the Zionist clarion, I find myself in agreement with Dr. Karpf on this point.
> ... Should the organization of such a [non-Zionist Jewish] body be indefinitely delayed, the A.J.C. might find itself

---

153 Horkheimer was part of the social sciences research department the AJC had assembled to answer the question of how to combat antisemitism:
This mission was of particular importance to John Slawson, Ph.D., who initiated the project. He constantly spoke of antisemitism as an "emotional disease" in search of the right antitoxin.
...[The AJC's scientific department] "evolved into a semipermanent organization producing a series of studies, including the landmark Studies in Prejudice, *which consisted of five massive volumes. The last of these volumes,* The Authoritarian Personality, *published in late 1949, became perhaps the most well known."*
—Marianne Rachel Sanua, *Let us prove strong: the American Jewish Committee,1945-2006*, Brandeis University Press, 2007, page 49.

154 Executive director, Federation of Jewish Welfare Organizations, Los Angeles.

> *have (sic) to proclaim its position publicly in order to protect American Judaism against being identified with Zionism.... any critical statement coming directly from the A.J.C. would, in the eyes of many uninformed Jews, only serve to identify us with the Council for Judaism.*
>
> *On the other hand, an independent non-Zionist body would also be free to affirm... its active interest in the development of Palestine. It could, to some extent at least, collaborate with those Zionists who are interested generally in resolving the Jewish cause...rather than furthering their own nationalistic philosophies. Thus this agency might prove to be a rung in our ladder to the ultimate goal of unity.*[155]

---

[155] "Dr. Max Horkheimer to Dr. Samuel Flowerman regarding the Berkeley Study," November 17, 1945, attachment to Horkheimer letter to Flowerman, ajcarchives.org.

"This miasma of Jewish unity."

IN THE September 1946 meeting, Maurice B. Hexter related a history of negotiations in which he had been involved, in which the Zionist Organization missed opportunities to accept agreements.

> Now if this invitation comes from the British Government and with the approval of the State Department and we go there, in my judgment we should be, as Judge Proskauer has indicated, moderate because we will get less tomorrow than we get today. The very thing that [Nahum] Goldmann now would give his ten fingers to get, Goldmann's party rejected at Zurich[at the Twentieth Zionist Congress in 1937, which rejected the Peel Commission proposal of a Jewish state in part of Palestine]. I was present and I know.[156]
>
> [Hexter recommends] ...that we separate and perhaps I may be misunderstood, we separate the problem of Palestine from the problem of the refugee.[157]

> ...I repeat, there is no problem that I can understand that invokes and has the right to command peoples' work more than this problem in Palestine. And if the Committee is invited, and if anything that I know can be of service to the Committee, nothing that I know or do should stand in the way.
>
> I hope that this Committee will, if it cannot take a different position from the established position in this hotel, the famous Biltmore Resolution, remain silent and really say that this is not an American Jewish Committee job. I would wish to add from my knowledge of some knowledge of the Arab situation which I think I have kept fairly well in contact, that if there is to be an imposed solution as indeed I fear we shall have to have, then I think it is important for us, as American citizens, to appreciate the statement that it is not alone by philanthropic contributions or by advice that this problem is to be solved. If there is to be an imposed solution, I think that we must follow the logic of the consequences, which is that we may have to send American troops there to help impose it.[158]

---

156 September 15, 1946 executive committee transcript, page 16-19, AJC.
157 Page 19, ibid.
158 Page 20, ibid.

While the Zionist goal was to achieve a majority in a political state, Hexter was willing to conceive of a Jewish minority status:

> DR. HEXTER: I have long held the view that the only solution is an agreed solution, and the longer we delay that agreement the less we would get. I would prefer an agreement with the Arabs, even a lesser agreement than I would get from the British Government, because I have no faith in bayonets even when they are in the hands of the British Tommie, whom I completely respect, as some of you know.
>
> Second, failing that, I prefer a solution along the lines of what, for lack of a better term, I would call bi-nationalism, under which I understand the following: A state which neither party controls, with emigration so geared that the Arabs will never fear being majorized (sic) by the Jews, which may involve our formal and perpetual abrogation of majority.
>
> CHAIRMAN BLAUSTEIN: You feel too that if the invitation is extended that we should reserve freedom and that we should be moderate and give the Jewish Agency the clearance to try to work this thing out?
>
> DR. HEXTER: Not alone freedom of action but not bound by this miasma of Jewish unity.
>
> CHAIRMAN BLAUSTEIN: And that if this does not work out, then you are for want of a better plan in favor of a bi-national state?
>
> DR. HEXTER: Yes. Roughly, that is correct.[159]

---

[159] Page 22, *ibid*.

"They are not our enemies."

The danger of regarding Arab, anti-partition forces as "enemies" in AJC discussions was noted in the May 1948 committee meeting transcript by Dr. Hans Kohn[*], as he warned that a previous speaker

> by implication at least, and I would very much deprecate such an implication as the most dangerous, spoke as if our enemies -- and by our enemies he could only mean Jewish enemies -- would oppose a Jewish state in Palestine.
>
> Ladies and gentlemen, that is simply not true. Many people who are far from being anti-semites, on the contrary who wish because they are not anti-semites, the assimilation the Jews into all the peoples of the American people, are opposing a Jewish state.
>
> Now another thing that was said which I think is a mistake, and should this report ever be published in minutes I would suggest that this error be removed, as I heard the report it referred to an Arab delegate at the United Nations as our enemy. I don't know whose enemy; not my enemy. He may be against a Jewish state; he is not the enemy of the Jews. He may be an anti-semite, as there are some in America and not only in Arab lands, they are in America, too. But not because he represents the Arab states at the present at the United Nations.
>
> We in Palestine have to live with Arabs in any foreseeable future.
>
> They may be against a Jewish state -- and I am against a Jewish state. They are not our enemies. Our, in the sense of the Jewish people and the American Jewish Committee, and I would suggest that this phrase should this report be incorporated in the minutes be eliminated.
>
> And what I plead for is that we learn that we have to live with the Arabs whether we like it or not. That for any foreseeable future the Jewish autonomous community in Palestine will be within an immense Arab territory, and those Arabs are today backward. They are immensely backward compared with the Jewish

---

[*] Prague-born Hans Kohn (1891-1971) taught history at City College and the New School for Social Research, and was the author of *The Idea of Nationalism: A Study in Its Origins and Background*, 1944.

> community. They may not be so in twenty or thirty or
> forty years' time though. Things change and backward
> peoples all over the world get less backward. And in
> twenty or thirty years' time it may be an entirely
> different situation in Palestine.[160]

The passage Kohn refers to seems to be in a report by Carl J. Austrian, regarding Zionist publicity in the USA.

> *Two impressions are immediately formed by those American citizens who are not identified with people in the Holy Land or with people desiring to live in that country. For one, they raise the criticism that Jews are using tax-exempt money to finance a struggle against the best interests of the United States.*
>
> *Rightly or wrongly, they feel that that action is against the best interests of the United States. And our enemies are very quick to take advantage of those things.*
>
> *This week at Lake Success, Jamal Husseini on behalf of the Arab High Committee speaking before the Political and Security Committee of the General Assembly, in answer to a Jewish Agency spokesman said, "I suppose, also, that he is well aware of the tax-exempt drive of the United Jewish Appeal of $250,000,000 that are being collected for this same invasion of Palestine."*
>
> *This opinion is given foundation by ads inserted by extremists in our daily press, to recruit American youth for Palestine warfare -- notwithstanding the imminence of universal military training in this country, and the fact that by such an act of enlistment an American Jew in effect renounces his American citizenship....*
>
> *Secondly, Jews are left open to the accusation that they are not interested in fund-raising appeals other than their own.*[161]

Dr. Nelson Glueck[*] of Cincinnati spoke in favor of an American approach to human relations:

> *I might say that those principles and those conditions which must prevail to enable the sustenance and the safety and the survival of Jews in Palestine and*

---

160 May 1-2, 1948 executive committee meeting transcript, page 84, box "EXECUTIVE COMMITTEE / TRANSCRIPTS / OCT. 1947-OCT. 1949," AJC.
161 Page 23, *ibid.*
* Rabbi and archaeologist, president of Hebrew Union College, Cincinnati.

elsewhere are exactly those principles which will enable our country, America, to endure and to survive....[162]

Kohn seconded Glueck's approach,
Dr. Hans Kohn: I entirely support Dr. Glueck that there is no future whatsoever with all the guns of the world, with all the blood and iron, there is no future unless we have collaboration with the Arabs. And if we spent one-tenth to influence the British and then influence Moscow, one-tenth of the money, of the energy, of the devotion, of the intelligence, in exploring at least the Arab field, we would be much farther than we are.[163]

Kohn's recommendation of cooperation with Arab national goals contrasts with the report of Sir Ronald Storrs in his 1937 memoir, that the British intention was that Palestine would form "for England 'a little loyal Jewish Ulster' in a sea of potentially hostile Arabism."[164]

Glueck applauded small contributions totaling $10,000 that AJC made to Dr. Judah Magnes in Jerusalem to support efforts for rapprochement between Jews and Arabs in Palestine.
As one who has lived in Palestine I think one of the sorriest records of Jewish endeavor there has been the long and continued and, on the whole, absolute failure to integrate Jewish life there with Arab life and to make the economy of the country one integral and indivisible part.[165]

(In a 1939 memo, Louis Brandeis is described as saying — on Arab-Jewish relations — "He felt that while [Jewish] Palestinians talked a great deal about it, they did nothing actually. There was a special need for our people to learn Arabic to mingle with the general population and to support and to improve our own Arabic press."[166])

Later, in the flush of the creation of the state, in September 1949 Israeli UN delegate Aubrey S. (Abba) Eban obliquely wrote in *Commentary*:
That Arab-Jewish agreement is a Jewish interest may be held a self-evident truth....even if its efforts to vindicate it

---

162 Page 52, *ibid.*
163 Page 82, *ibid.*
164 *The Memoirs of Sir Ronald Storrs*, G.P. Putnam's Sons, New York, 1937, page 364.
165 May 1-2, 1948 transcript, page 52.
166 "MEMORANDUM," [Handwritten at top:] "11/29/39," Isadore Breslau Papers; P-507; box 1; folder 1, AJHS.

> *often lacked the conviction and tenacity which were usually devoted to other agreed Zionist objectives.*[167]

Discussing Magnes and his Ehud group, which had been for a negotiated, bi-national state, Eban said:
> *The doctrine of "established fact" has been entirely vindicated against that of "prior consent."*[168]

Eban's nimble essay argued that that Israeli statehood was accomplished the way it had to be done, "vindicated" by the fact that it was done. *Commentary* noted, "This is his first published article in an American magazine." It was the start of a brilliant career presenting Israel's position in American media.

The AJC apprehension at a Jewish State's imminent creation is illustrated in this poem's stanza, delivered at the January 1948 Annual Meeting:
> *Mankind, unnerved by clashing world disorders,*
>   *Beset by hungry plea and dying groan,*
> *Has little need of new dividing borders*
>   *Enclosing nations striving for their own.*[169]

---

[167] Aubrey S. Eban, "The Future of Arab-Jewish Relations", *Commentary*, September 1949, page 200.
[168] Page 203, *ibid*.
[169] Herbert B. Ehrmann, AJC Vice President, "To the Jewish State", 41st Annual Report of the American Jewish Committee, page 137. Annual Meeting of the AJC was held at the Hotel Commodore, New York City, Jan. 16-18, 1948

The AJC and Jews in the Arab Countries: "We consider the lives of the Jews of Yemen and of Egypt no less important than Jewish lives in Palestine."

..... At the time of Israeli independence, Jewish immigration to Palestine had been 86.7% Ashkenazim(355,117), 6.6% Sephardim (27,724), and 3.8% Yemenites(15,430).[170] This was before the vast disruption of life of the Jewish communities in Arab countries, a phenomenon the AJC foresaw as a consequence of Palestine partition. The report of the staff subcommittee on the Near East observes that in the Islamic-majority countries of the Near East and North Africa,

It was emphasized that the Jewish problems there are of a specific nature and that in view of the forthcoming partition of Palestine, the position of the Jewish communities in the Near East would be aggravated and would certainly call for intervention on their behalf.[171]

A January 1948 AJC memo to the American Friends Service Committee estimates 700,000 Jews in Arab countries, and 900,000 in all Muslim countries. It surveys hazards in popular sentiment and government actions in the months subsequent to partition, and asks the AFSC "to secure the information desired and consequently to extend, through its representatives, its assistance and help to the Jews in the Arab countries of the Near East whose safety is now jeopardized."[172]

A March 1948 *Commentary* article on the pending Partition does note the danger for Arab-world Jews, and asks, "And who, incidentally, will protect the 800,000 non-Palestinian Jews of the Middle East and North Africa in the event of a *jihad*?"[173]

The intensified settling of "Arab Palestine" by European Jews was noted throughout the Arab world, and one newspaper in Morocco angrily noted the United Jewish Appeal division of funds which by formula allocated a majority to Palestine projects, in a translation provided to the AJC by the francophone Alliance Israelite:

There are organizations in Morocco which work for

---

[170] AJYB, Vol.50.
[171] "The Report of the Subcommittee on the Near East", January 23, 1948, in "The Record of the American Jewish Committee in RE Palestine," Vol. 4, AJC.
[172] "The Present Status of the Jews in the Arab Countries," *ibid*.
[173] *Commentary Magazine*, vol. 5, no 3, March 1948, page 213.

> *Palestine and collect money in the purpose to fight against Arabs....Poor and rich contribute to this collect; and most of the Jews say that these sums are destined for indigent population; still actually they send 2/3 of it to Palestine and 1/3 they keep for their poors.*[174]

The AJC had not accepted the rationale of "ingathering."
> *We have never seen the interests of Diaspora Jewry as in opposition to those of Eretz Israel; conversely, we can hardly be expected to accept the elevation on a priority basis of the fate of the Jews of Eretz Israel over that of Diaspora Jewry. We consider the lives of the Jews of Yemen and of Egypt no less important than Jewish lives in Palestine; and the fact that Agency policy and Palestine events can have an important bearing on the lives of Jews in the United States, as well as in the other Western democracies must also guide our thinking.*[175]

A CIA report forecast the disaster to come:
> *Before the enunciation of the Balfour Declaration in 1917, the Jews in the Near East fared as well as other minority groups throughout the world. Since 1917, however, they have had to bear the brunt of Arab antagonism to the development of political Zionism in Palestine. In the event of partition, the lives of the million Jews throughout the Arab world (including Palestine) will be imperiled...--as illustrated at the time of the Baghdad revolt in 1941 when the Jewish quarter was attacked. A representative of the Jewish Agency has stated that in the event of partition the 400,000 Jews in the Arab states outside Palestine may have to be sacrificed in the interest of the Jewish community as a whole.*[176]

---

174 "Translation of Moroccan newspaper article, 'The Zionist Poison in Morocco,'" Joel D. Wolfsohn to Foreign Affairs Department, letter Aug. 29, 1947, with attachment, ajcarchives.org

175 "Notes for a Non-Zionist Palestine Policy for American Jews," Feb. 11, 1948, page 3, "The Record of the American Jewish Committee in RE Palestine," Vol. 3, AJC.

176 " The Consequences of the Partition of Palestine," Nov. 28, 1947, www.foia.cia.gov, page 7.

"No room can be made in Palestine for a second nation except by dislodging or exterminating."

THE AJC was acutely aware of the conflict between the 1943 Biltmore agenda for a Jewish state, and the demographic realities in Palestine. Their assumption was that Jewish emigration could and must continue, in some form of accommodation with Arab Palestinians.

In the warfare already simmering in Palestine at the time of Blaustein's speech, a majority of Arab residents would become refugees outside the actual borders (the 1949 armistice line) of the new Jewish state. The AJC had envisioned a different outcome:

> *The Jewish State will not be a national state. Although its primary aim will be to enlarge the Jewish population by an increased immigration, it will in fact, if not in theory, be a bi-national state. With a large Arab minority (over 400,000 Arabs among 550,000 Jews), the Jewish state will strictly adhere to the democratic principles and protection of minorities, in view of the fact that independence is to be granted to a Jewish state in Palestine on recommendation and under the auspices of the United Nations.*[177]

Blaustein, Morris Waldman, and Edward Warburg of the AJC were present in a May 1941 meeting where Chaim Weizmann said there must be Palestinian Arab resettlement, in order for the Zionist vision to be properly realized. Weizmann explained that at the proper time, "when the world has quieted down," it could be explained to Arab statesmen, "We are there; we have to be there." Land in Trans-Jordan or Iraq would be purchased to which Arabs would be moved.[178]

In November 1939, Louis Brandeis is quoted by Isadore Breslau as objecting to a planned visit to the United States by Weizmann: "He believed the whole thing was a mistake. He was afraid Weizmann would press his plan for political action, based on a future re-shuffling of populations."[179]

---

[177] "Palestine Staff Committee," AJC, Nov. 17, 1947, page 1, RG347.7.1, Box 78, folder "AJC Staff Meeting", YIVO.
[178] Rafael Medoff, *Zionism and the Arabs: an American Jewish dilemma, 1898-1948*, Praeger, 1997, page 105.
[179] "MEMORANDUM," [Handwritten at top:] "11/29/39," Isadore Breslau Papers; P-507; box 1; folder 1; AJHS.

In a February 1940 meeting with President Roosevelt, Weizmann is reported to have said that "of course they (Jews) would compensate the Arabs in a reasonable way for anything they got." He said the Arabs "had completely failed in their efforts to dislodge the Jews. That was a fact which was likely to have a fundamental effect on future relations with the Arabs. Already there were signs - he was not going to exaggerate them, but they were unmistakable - that the Arabs realizing their failure were casting around to see if they could not arrive at some modus vivendi." This followed President Roosevelt asking, "What about the Arabs? Can't that be settled with a little baksheesh?" Weizmann "said it wasn't as simple as all that."[180]

There was no shortage of counsel against the maximal goals of Zionist state-making. I.F. Stone noted in his first visit to Palestine in a Nov. 24, 1945 column that "The sense of consecration and human effort in the Jewish community must powerfully attract all who prize human courage, devotion, and idealism."

Stone went on to say,
> *political agreement will be impossible so long as a single Jewish state in Palestine is demanded.*
> *We have been carrying on a campaign in America on the basis of half-truths, and on this basis no effective politics can be waged, and no secure life built for Yishuv.*[181]

As Brandeis[182] had in 1915, Stone in a December 8, 1945, report from Palestine saluted Zionists as an analogue to America's Puritans:
> *Only a passionate, narrow, and mystical national faith made it possible for Jews to colonize areas the goats despised. Without the Zionist movement, what has been achieved in Palestine would never have come to pass. The closest parallel in American life is Puritanism, and Palestine is indeed like the frontiers in our own country, both in Colonial times and in the West. But the strength*

---

[180] "Memorandum of Conversation Between Y.C. and P., Feb. 8th, 1:00 P.M.," Isadore Breslau Papers, P-507, box 2, folder 11, AJHS. The memorandum is sent with a cover note to Breslau by Arthur Lourie. A similar or identical account of the meeting is cited in Michael T. Benson, *Harry S. Truman and the Founding of Israel*, as "Note of Conversation between President Roosevelt, Dr. Chaim Weizmann, and Lord Lothian, Washington, D.C., 8 February 1940," in the Central Zionist Archives, Z4 15463.
[181] "Jewry in a Blind Alley," Nov. 24, 1945, *The Best of I.F. Stone*, Public Affairs, New York, 2006, page 210.
[182] Brandeis refers to "These new Pilgrim Fathers," *Zionism and Patriotism*, Federation of American Zionists, 1915, page 2.

associated with such a movement also has its corresponding defects, and the defects of Zionism are its failure to take into account the feelings and aspirations of the Palestinian Arab....The Arab does not fear the Jew, but he fears being dominated by him, and this fear must be allayed.[183]

The CIA noted in 1947, that "many [American] Zionist organizations, while supporting the objectives of a National Home for Jews, do not advocate an independent Jewish nation in Palestine."[184]

A 1930 American magazine article contains exasperation familiar to us now:

Some long-drawn struggles make us weary—the endless cross-pulling of patent self-interests. Some enlist our chivalry, as cases of right against might. Some command a deeper concern—the conflict of two rights, two equally justifiable ideals, which the facts somehow have made incompatible; these contain the essence of tragedy, for without sacrifice on one side, or on both, there is no solution. This is the case in Palestine, for here are two corporate streams of hope which we rudely describe as 'national,' each with a valid claim on our sympathy, while both cannot be realized. And no political power dares deny either the right to life.[185]

George Antonius wrote in the widely-read book *The Arab Awakening*(1939),

Once the fact is faced that the establishment of a Jewish state in Palestine, or of a national home based on territorial sovereignty, cannot be accomplished without forcibly displacing the Arabs, a way to solution becomes clearer....The renunciation will not be easy. Jewish hopes have been raised to such a pitch that the non-fulfillment of the Zionist dream of a Jewish state in Palestine will cause intense disillusionment and bitterness. The manifold proofs of public spirit and of capacity to endure hardships and face danger in the building up of the national home are there to testify to

---

[183] Stone, ibid, p216-217.
[184] "The Consequences of the Partition of Palestine," Nov. 28, 1947, www.foia.cia.gov, page 16.
[185] William Ernest Hocking, "Palestine: An Impasse?", *Atlantic*, June 1930.

> the devotion with which a large section of the Jewish people cherish the Zionist ideal. And it would be an act of further cruelty to the Jews to disappoint those hopes if there existed some way of satisfying them, that did not involve cruelty to another people. But the logic of facts is inexorable. It shows that no room can be made in Palestine for a second nation except by dislodging or exterminating the nation in possession.[186]

---

[186] George Antonius, *The Arab Awakening, The Story of the Arab National Movement*, J.B. Lippincott, Philadelphia, 1939, page 410-412.

"It was originally a straddling document, and its amendment would probably lead to additional straddling."

The endorsement of a Partition plan for Palestine in 1946 culminated — and ended — an AJC position, since the Balfour declaration, of non-Zionism, while cooperating with Zionist organizations.

The hope to be an organization that could work with both Zionists and anti-Zionists did not mean that there was not a definite distaste in AJC for assumptions underlying Herzl and modern Jewish nationalism. As AJC president Judge Joseph Proskauer wrote to Undersecretary of State Stettinius in 1944,

> *My group is deeply concerned over the efforts of the World Jewish Congress and its allies to promulgate what is called the nationalist theory of Jewish Life. Envisaging Jews as exiles and a diaspora. We think this is a false and dangerous doctrine.*[187]

Perhaps the 1948 speech is a "straddle" again, as was the 1918 statement regarding the Balfour Declaration. In the speech, Blaustein states that the AJC recommended to UNSCOP in 1947 a UN trusteeship, but if an ultimate political solution must be found, that partition was the AJC's choice, to accomplish Jewish immigration to Palestine of homeless Jews.

In January 1943, outgoing AJC President Maurice Wertheim, explained the proposed Committee "Statement of Views" on Palestine was an attempt to work toward harmony with the American Zionists — "The objective is joint action and not a joint ideology."[188] The 1943 statement was a restatement and updating of the 1918 statement —

> *"We recognize that there are now more than half a million Jews in Palestine who have built up a sound and flourishing economic life and a satisfying spiritual and cultural life, and who now constitute substantially one-third of the population...settlement in Palestine although an important factor, cannot alone furnish and*

---

[187] Proskauer to Edward R. Stettinius, Jr., Feb. 18, 1944, box 4.65, file jj-2-104 Stettinius, JHU.
[188] Address of Maurice Wertheim, AJC 1943 Annual Meeting, AJYB, Vol. 45, page 636.

> should not be expected to furnish the solution of
> the problem of post-war Jewish rehabilitation.

— again rejecting the idea that Palestine was to be the singular future home of a Jewish nation.

In May 1944, the AJC Palestine committee reported,
> The failure of the American Jewish Committee to speak either for or against the Jewish Commonwealth, <u>resulted in a virtual declaration of war upon the American Jewish Committee by the Zionists</u>. Mr. [David] Sher pointed out, however, that the phrase Jewish Commonwealth, that is so frequently bandied about, has yet to be defined; even such a student of foreign affairs as [Under Secretary of State] Sumner Welles, after devoting considerable praise to the policies pursued by the Zionists under the leadership of Chaim Weizmann, concludes with an endorsement of the position of Dr. Magnes, which is completely antithetical to that held by Chaim Weizmann officially....
> Mr. [Maurice] Wertheim said that he did not think it at all feasible to attempt further clarification of the 1943 Statement because it was originally a straddling document, and its amendment would probably lead to additional straddling. Mr. Sher then proposed that the American Jewish Committee might avow the position of neutrality taken by the B'nai Brith at their last convention in May, 1944.
> At this point a draft of a statement, prepared by Judge Proskauer, was also read...that the "American Jewish Committee has never set itself up as an agency to propagandize the ultimate anti-Zionist position or the ultimate Zionist position."
> Mr. Sher...suggested that it would be useful to hold additional meetings to explore the 'neutrality' issue further."[189]

As part of the AJC's continuous involvement and cooperation with the Jewish Agency, the Committee issued this press release on a July 2, 1946 visit by Blaustein and John Slawson to Henry F. Grady(for Secretary of State Byrnes) and Goldthwaite H. Dorr (for Secretary of War Patterson),

---

[189] Minutes, Meeting of AJC Palestine Committee, Dec. 19, 1944, 3 pages, in "The Record of the American Jewish Committee in RE Palestine." Vol. 1, AJC. Emphasis added.

members of President Truman's special cabinet committee on Palestine, before their departure for London to discuss Palestine issues with British government officials.

> *The British Administration has sought to justify its conduct by describing it as an attempt to restore law and order in the face of violence by certain extremist elements in the Jewish community. The American Jewish Committee associates itself entirely with all the responsible leaders of Palestinian Jewry who have unanimously condemned any resort to terror. At the same time, the Committee must emphasize that the chief cause of the unrest among the Jewish population of Palestine is the British refusal to admit 100,000 displaced European Jews into Palestine... Not until the British Government has put an end to its dilatory policy will it be able to create in Palestine an environment unfavorable to violence, or do justice to the Jews still languishing in displaced persons' camps fourteen months after Hitler's downfall.*[190]

The King David Hotel bombing by the Irgun followed on July 22, 1946, as part of guerrilla warfare waged in Palestine by the Irgun (and the Lehi, the "Stern Gang") against the British Army, and continued throughout the next year. June 30, 1947, the bodies of two British sergeants were found hanging in a eucalyptus grove near Natanya.[191]

The AJC saw itself as the "honest broker" who could moderate extreme Zionists and transmute their fervor into cooperation with the British and Arabs, as Proskauer "anticipates progress" Aug. 20, 1946 in a planned conference:

> *...negotiations are in progress for conferences between the British Government, the Jewish Agency and the Arab States, which will be of the deepest and most determinative consequence....*
> *Rancor, bitterness, vituperation and schism must be banished from our thinking and our conduct at*

---

[190] Press Release, July 2, 1946, Vol. 1, *ibid.*
[191] "Their bloodied, blackened bodies swung to & fro from eucalyptus trees. Their shirts were wrapped around their heads. Through their clothes and flesh were pinned Irgun 'communiqués' accusing the sergeants of 'anti-Jewish crimes.' They had died slowly, by clumsy strangulation. The terrorists had added a distinctive touch; they had booby-trapped one of their victims." *Time* magazine, Aug. 11, 1947.

this critical moment. Chauvinism must moderate its excesses and appeal to violence must cease. This is no time for either bomb or bombast. If the Jewish Agency will adhere to the principles above suggested and can negotiate a plan acceptable to the British and the Arabs along these lines, it will certainly have taken a long step forward.[192]

---

[192] Statement by Joseph M. Proskauer, August 20, 1946, RECORD OF THE AJC IN RE PALESTINE, Vol. 1, AJC.

"The only difference between Judge Lazansky and myself is a matter of emphasis."

In 1947, the May 11 executive committee discussion of Palestine options begins with a report of Judge Proskauer, which includes his observation, "You cannot have what is called a Jewish State in any sense in a country which is two-thirds Arab. That is a plain, inescapable proposition. Therefore, if you want a Jewish State in any form there is a condition precedent to that, and that is immigration into Palestine."

Proskauer discussed in detail how the AJC intended to cooperate with the Jewish Agency, and Zionist and other organizations in their goal of continuing "infiltration" of Jewish immigrants into Palestine, but preferred trusteeship to near-term independence or partition.

> With respect to partition, let me say I said before the Anglo-American Committee that we had to remember that Palestine was a country with is the size of one of our smallest states and to divide it up carried certain very grave difficulties; and that I very much hoped that there could be a solution beyond that.

Proskauer, after describing trying to give tactical advice to the Jewish Agency, said,

> I have had some people suggest that we ought to follow the course which has been followed by the [American] Council for Judaism and come out in the newspapers with periodical denunciations of the Jewish Agency and of its work. I, for one, shall engage in no such enterprise. I need not elaborate to you the reasons which actuate one to such a decision. ...
> I am not criticizing the Council for Judaism. God knows, I am not fighting with them. Many of them are members of this group and many of them are my dearest friends. I do think that as a practical pragmatic political program that it is an error to keep asserting one's hundred per cent Americanism on every possible occasion. I think it is a little bit like the lady who assured us that she is virtuous; and I am not proposing to engage in newspaper controversy with the Agency or to make newspaper statements....

The executive committee solicited opinions on Palestine from AJC chapter executive committees. Philadelphia's position was the AJC position: trusteeship first, partition only if necessary.

St Louis:
> *"The basic points of view of the executive committee of the St. Louis Chapter are strongly in opposition to Jewish Nationalism and political Zionism. We regard Palestine strictly from the humanitarian point of view, namely, as one among other countries, including the United States, where refugees seek asylum. Any policy which furthers these beliefs will meet with our whole-hearted approval...."*

St. Louis chairman Singer goes on to object to an AJC April 29 statement favoring the Jewish Agency's application for representation at the UN's Palestine sessions on a non-voting basis.
> *I feel, and I am sure that several of my associates concur, that this statement implies a recognition of Jewish Nationalism, or, in other words, the status of Jews as members of a national rather than a religious group. JUDGE PROSKAUER: If you will let me interrupt a minute, that is just plain nonsense. They did not appear as a member; they were not recognized in any way excepting to appear and state their views.*

Boston, statement of chairman, Mr. Ehrmann:
> *The Committee is handling the Palestine issue in a wise and statesmanlike fashion....With reference to Palestine, we are in agreement with the statement of views originally adopted by the Committee on January 1, 1943. We feel that in the United Nations position the American Jewish Committee should do everything in its power toward the primary end of realizing the abrogation of the White Paper of 1939 in allowing free an unlimited immigration and acquisition of land.*

New Orleans:
> *These five men are in full accord with the general policy of the AJC, as expressed in the statement of policy of January, 1946....*
> *If the officers believe that partition of Palestine is the best*

way to achieve this end, then we recommend that the officers support partition.

The San Francisco executive committee prepared a full memorandum on its own initiative. It contains suggestions of the basis of approach, goals and methods. Excerpts from the memorandum:

Caution: Whatever views the AJC may finally reach after reappraisal and rethinking, it should not throw its weight against any settlement more favorable to Zionist views, if such a settlement appears likely to be adopted.

Conversely, it ought not actively to espouse any plan not in accord with the best judgment in the hope of uniting divergent groups.

Finally, if by taking an active position it will increase acrimony among Jews and impair its usefulness in other fields without contributing to a solution, the AJC should bow out of the Palestine problem and confine its attention to other matters.

Goals: There are two, and only two, goals to be attained. One, the Jewish population of Palestine must be fully protected in their persons, property and cultural existence. Two, Jewish immigration into Palestine must be free until the displaced Jews have been drained from Europe to Palestine and elsewhere.

This goal means (a) the immediate admission of 100,000, and (b) the later and more gradual admission of others. There may be, perhaps, an additional 100,000 to 200,000.

Method: If the two goals suggested are adopted, the method and machinery for attaining and preserving them are secondary and may be left to the national officers and the professional staff of the AJC who deal with the problem from day to day. The following, however is suggested.

One: Discussion about a Jewish State should cease.

Two: Something in the nature of the British (Bevin) plan should be adopted.

Three: Protection of Jewish rights may require the maintenance of a balance between Jews and Arabs by external sanction or by an outside power.

Four: The Jewish Agency should be replaced by some other body or thoroughly recruited so that it ceases to be simply a Zionist body.

William Weiss noted an ambiguity in a proposed AJC resolution to urge the General Assembly as soon as possible that the Mandatory Government authorize the immediate admission of 100,000 Jews into Palestine — "nowhere does it say 'displaced' by the way." This was the crux of the difference between "soft" Zionism and Herzlian Zionism — whether Palestine was to be haven for "displaced," homeless Jews, or more generally a regathering of world Jews.

After Edward Lazansky spoke at length for explicit AJC support of partition, Judge Proskauer said,

> *I do not find myself in disagreement at all about his ultimates. I find him in agreement with me that, of course, in the presentation of this specific issue before the United Nations, it is impossible to go in and ask that Palestine be made a Jewish state as a whole at a time when two-thirds of its population is Arab. I take it that there could be no dissent from that proposition. The only difference between Judge Lazansky and myself is a matter of emphasis. Let me assume, at least, that we see eye to eye on the proposal that we envisage a state in Palestine, a democratic state, Jewish only in the sense that the Jews have a majority, and in other respects a completely democratic state -- as Judge Stern pointed out in his article, from which you read.** *Let me assume, arguendo, at least that that is our common objective; and suppose, if you please, that we were both attorneys for the Jewish Agency, seeking to get that kind of state in Palestine. That really is, I take it, the area of difference between us.*
> *Palestine is a country of the area of, approximately, Rhode Island, I believe.*
> *MR. [Edward A.] NORMAN: No, Vermont.*
> *JUDGE PROSKAUER: Well, one of the smaller states. It is very closely knitted together economically. There are certain very grave objections, from the point of view of the Jew, to partition. I advocated it last summer, as I told you ad hoc, because I thought it had a possibility of a quick short-cut to what Judge Lazansky has in his mind. But I have never been blind to the dangers of it.*
> *Surely, -- I am going to use the words "Jewish State" as a shorthand term to describe this kind of state that Judge Stern spoke of -- surely it would be the tiniest of states. It would be surrounded in the immediate entourage by, if I*

---

* See summary of article, Page 130-131.

> *remember the figure correctly, some seventy million Arabs. It would have to depend for its sustenance and for its prosperity on the closest economic relations with the Arab state that would be created and the other Arab states that are around it. And it would always be sitting, the tiniest of commonwealths, endangered by the hostility of surrounding countries....*
>
> *Now let us look at the picture which would be presented if we could really get a United Nations trusteeship...and it is all a question of timing. If five years from now we will have infiltrated into Palestine even half a million Jews, if we are fortunate and can infiltrate into Palestine 700,000 Jews, then you could go to the United Nations, and with our joint objective in mind, Judge Lazansky, ask for the recognition of Palestinian independence along the lines that Judge Stern set forth. And I hold the profound conviction that wisdom, foresight and statesmanship -- statesmanship from the Zionist point of view -- make it wholly advisable that at least one Jewish organization should strongly present to the United Nations that aspect of the problem.*
>
> *...And I should find myself most embarrassed if I had to go in before the United Nations Committee of Inquiry and say our insistence is on partition or nothing.*
>
> *I present a much better picture for the Jews of Palestine, for the Jews of the world, if I say: "We have waited this long, we have infiltrated 600,000 Jews into Palestine, insure us the opportunity of infiltrating more and then give us a state. If you cannot do that and give us this bigger state, this state of the whole of Palestine, then at least give us this tiny morsel of a partition state."*[93]

A February 8, 1948 handwritten note in preparation for a meeting of Proskauer and Blaustein with President Harry S. Truman read:

> *As you know org AJC is composed of a most representative cross-section of Am Jewry-*
> *-& is non-Z, not Z*
> *originally preferred no political solution of Pal at this time*[194]

---

[193] May 10-11, 1947 Executive Committee Transcript, Archive box "EXECUTIVE COMMITTEE / TRANSCRIPTS / OCT. 1943-MAY 1947", pages 34, 53, 58, 70-77, 102, 124, AJC.

[194] Handwritten notes, " JB/PRO—Truman," Feb. 8, 1948, Box 2.21, C-2-23 "Proskauer, Judge Joseph M.," JHU.

"We naturally move to those places where we are not persecuted, and there our presence produces persecution."

Publication of Jacob Blaustein's speech retrieves facts of 1946-48, and what AJC endorsement of partition did and did not mean. The AJC in no sense endorsed Theodor Herzl's Zionist premise: that Jews were to "get out" from the non-Jewish world where they were not welcome, and create a political home in Palestine. Herzl wrote:

> We naturally move to those places where we are not persecuted, and there our presence produces persecution. This is the case in every country, and will remain so, even in those highly civilized--for instance, France--until the Jewish question finds a solution on a political basis. The unfortunate Jews are now carrying the seeds of Anti-Semitism into England; they have already introduced it into America. ...
>
> In countries which now are Anti-Semitic my view will be approved. In others, where Jews now feel comfortable, it will probably be violently disputed by them. My happier co-religionists will not believe me till Jew-baiting teaches them the truth; for the longer Anti-Semitism lies in abeyance the more fiercely will it break out. The infiltration of immigrating Jews, attracted to a land by apparent security, and the ascent in the social scale of native Jews, combine powerfully to bring about a revolution. Nothing is plainer than this rational conclusion. ...
>
> Everything tends, in fact, to one and the same conclusion, which is clearly enunciated in that classic Berlin phrase: "Juden Raus!" (Out with the Jews!)[195]

The AJC had spent the 40 years of its existence vindicating the rights of Jews in America and throughout the world, and was undertaking new programs to fight employment and housing discrimination in the United States. Its support of the Universal Declaration of Human Rights — at the 1945 United Nations organizing conference in San Francisco, as part of the US delegation — was concerned with Jews as individuals. In June 1945, Blaustein spoke at Hunter College:

> At the time of Versailles, it was thought that the best

---

[195] Theodor Herzl, *Der Judenstaat*, 1896,
www.jewishvirtuallibrary.org/jsource/Zionism/herzl2.html

> *guarantee for the Jews of Eastern Europe where they were discriminated against, would be to secure national minority rights for them. But experience since then, like in Poland, for example, proved that in actual practice the minorities system is a failure and does not protect. It is clear, as our [AJC] Research Institute and Peace Problems Committee pointed out, that the best way to safeguard the interests of Jews in most situations -- there are some special exceptions -- is not to raise a Jewish issue but instead to work for a system which will protect all human beings, Jew included.*[196]

In contrast is this report of a speech by American Jewish Congress president Rabbi Stephen S. Wise in 1938:

> *Any Jew who speaks of "Americans who are Jews" is going back to the cowardice of the German Jews who spoke of themselves as German citizens of the Jewish faith, Dr. Wise continued, and the German Jews were woefully and tragically punished for their error.*[197]

Rabbi Elmer Berger had a different analysis in 1945, dissenting from the idea that the German Jewish experience discredited Jews living among others:

> *Germany, up to this time, has not used the modern heritage of the Western World. Jews, social-democrats, Heine, Goethe, Thomas Mann--all these and more and by no means Jews alone--were spewed out of a Germany that has not digested the substance of modern society in the last hundred years. Germany and its Jews and their tragedy taught us nothing we should not have known. It merely repeated the historic truth that where men are free, Jews live in security. Where they are not free, Jews, and others know no freedom.*
>
> *For it is not accurate to say that emancipation and integration were ever really tried in Germany. Emancipation did not fail, it was never real. The average Jew no more failed in Germany than Thomas Mann or Heinrich Brüning failed.*[198]

---

[196] Speech typescript, "6/26/45," Box 2.3, File A-2-6 Special-JB to San Francisco 1945, JHU.
[197] NY Herald Tribune, June 13, 1938, page 12.
[198] Rabbi Elmer Berger, *The Jewish Dilemma: The Case Against Zionist Nationalism*, Devin-Adair, New York, 1945, page 25.

Canadian poet Irving Layton gives a good example of the quandary about safety in which Jews may live, leading to a concept of the State of Israel as a "bolt hole" if needed:

> *High culture didn't stop thousands of refined opera-loving Germans, Poles, Hungarians, Czechs, Frenchmen from dipping their hands into the blood of the millions of Jews who had the tragic misfortune of living amongst them...The plain and simple truth that the Holocaust has made clear for us is that the Christianized world was tested and found wanting.*[199]

The conflict between Zionists and non-Zionists was bitter. After a contentious Dec. 18, 1940 meeting among American Jewish philanthropies regarding allocation of funds of the United Jewish Appeal, Rabbi Wise wrote Zionist publicist Isadore Breslau on United Palestine Appeal stationary:

> *...we are making a fight over the National Refugee Service as a partner. They plan to make this temporary exigency of refugeeism into a permanent problem of the Jewish people.* [added in pen:] *& put it on a parity with Palestine.*
>
> *I cannot write with any degree of patience or self-restraint. It is simply too awful.*[200]

Veteran Zionist Rabbi Abba Hillel Silver hailed Herzl in a sermon to his Cleveland, Ohio, congregation in 1960 as having summarized "simple axioms" about the "Jewish problem":

> *The Jew cannot be assimilated--some do, but the Jewish people does not. Neither persecution nor discriminatory law will solve the Jewish problem. Discrimination will make their position worse and the position of peoples around them--no better and perhaps worse. Granting the Jew political equality does not relieve anti-Semitism, and economic competition between the Jewish middle class and the non-Jewish middle class will lead to friction and bitterness against the Jewish minority. There is no solution simply in emigration, in infiltrating other countries. To do so would be merely to recreate that*

---

199 *Wild Gooseberries: The Selected Letters of Irving Layton,* Macmillan of Canada, Toronto, 1989, page 358-359.
200 "Meeting of Negotiating Committees" at UJA, December. 18, 1939, and December 22, 1939 letter, Isadore Breslau Papers; P-507; box 1; folder 10; AJHS. See Morocco newspaper where mingling of charitable and Palestine settlement funds was a grievance, page 107.

> same problem elsewhere. The solution to the Jewish problem lies in the establishment of a Jewish State and an organized emigration of the masses of Jewry to a territory given to them by charter where they can have self-government and control their own destinies.[201]

Unusually for a Reform rabbi, Silver in 1950 propounded a sort of Religious Zionist rationale for reëstablishment of a Jewish state:

> Exile made the mission of Israel impossible because the mission of a defeated people is automatically discredited. Exile was defeat for God as well as for Israel. ...The god of a defeated and conquered people has little to recommend Him.[202]

David Ben Gurion, then Chairman of the Jewish Agency, in 1944 summarized the Zionist program in "The Imperatives of the Jewish Revolution," a speech to youth leaders in Haifa:

> We must master our fate, we must take our destiny into our own hands! This is the doctrine of the Jewish revolution -- not non-surrender to the Dispersion [Galut] but making an end of it.
>
> Dispersion means dependence-material, political, spiritual, cultural, and intellectual dependence because we are aliens, a minority, bereft of a homeland, rootless and separated from the soil, from labor, and from basic industry. Our task is to break radically with this dependence and to become masters of our own fate - in a word, to achieve independence....
>
> I shall now say a few words in conclusion about the goal of our revolution: It is the complete ingathering of the exiles into a socialist Jewish state.[203]

---

[201] Abba Hillel Silver, "Theodor Herzl On the Occasion of the One-Hundredth Anniversary of His Birth," *A Word in Its Season*, World Publishing, New York, 1972, page 410.
[202] *Ibid*, page 383.
[203] http://zionism-israel.com/hdoc/Ben-Gurion_Jewish_revolution.htm

"The negation of Jewish life in the Galut...."

Elliot Cohen[*] in December 1947 enumerated a list of "Present-day Negative Attitudes Fostered by Jewish Nationalism" for the AJC, observing that "Many observers anticipate increasing nationalist and separatist interests, attitudes and ideologies in Jewish life.":

- *Concept of the homelessness of the Jew in the Western world. His perspective must be that of the alien and he can never hope to be more than that of a second-class citizen either in Europe or America.*
- *Anti-Semitism as a permanent reality in the Western world with the accompanying exaggeration of the universality, intensity and violence of anti-Semitism in the United States (every Gentile is an anti-Semite).*
- *The negation of Jewish life in the Galut....*
- *Minimization of the role of individual Jews in American life....*
- *A negative attitude to emancipation in which its threat and menace is constantly underscored.... freedom becomes the worst enemy of the survival of the Jewish group.*
- *Minimization of the character of the Western Jew. More than one writer has called our attention to the characterization of the Jew by nationalist propagandists which come very close to those of the anti-Semite. [Writings present that] A Jew is a luftmensch, a parasite, a trader, a non-producer, an intellectual, a neurotic; he has no roots in the soil; and by and large--due, of course, to no fault of his own--he is an undesirable personality generally. The rise of certain attitudes which represent a reversal of traditional Jewish values, for example, the present glorification of force and terrorism, and the spreading contempt for intellectual and cultural values. This transformation of values is what a number of Jewish thinkers have begun to refer to as the assimilationism of Jewish nationalism. ...We may be entering a period of nationalist Zealotism in America. What is more likely is that we are entering a period of emotional activity with which the average Jew will hold all kinds of conflicting, inconsistent ideas at the same time and present the spectacle of an emergency-driven*

---

* Elliot E. Cohen, editor of *Commentary* magazine, 1945-1959.

> *individual, neglectful of his Jewish cultural and religious obligations and of his American interests.*[204]

Mordecai Kosover speculated in November 1947, "There is the possibility that with the establishment of a Jewish State in Palestine, the Zionist movement all over the world will be dissolved. Its ultimate aim...achieved."[205]

However, in a January 1948 meeting of the AJC Committee on Palestine, it was suspected, "The Zionists will now make an attempt to organize the community along Zionist lines and will try to capture the communal organizations." Resistance was deprecated: "There is no chance of combating the expansionist policy of the ZOA. Although we reject the principle of nationalism in their program, we have to work with the Zionists in the areas of agreement."[206]

Kosover in December 1947 projected a Zionist goal of the rout of non-Zionism in the American Jewish community in his analysis, "Report on Zionist Thinking and Activities":

> *Zionism is to become the dominant movement in Jewish life and take up the position of indisputable leadership of Jewish forces everywhere, and thus it will organize and activate Jewish community life. The old Herzelian slogan: "Let's conquer the Jewish communities!" is going to be revived.... Now is the time for the Zionist movement to assume the hegemony over Jewish life in America through a variety of ways.*
>
> *Zionising the Jewish community of the United States will be the main task of the American Zionists to be carried out through the ZOA in conjunction with the Hadassah. The first step toward the accomplishment of this aim would be to formulate and announce a general policy of active participation in Jewish communal affairs. Following these tactics, Zionists everywhere could make their influence felt.*
>
> *This, Zionist leaders are of the opinion, could be done*

---

[204] Palestine Staff Committee, AJC, document "6. Cultural and Ideological Problems", pages numbered 4 and 5, pencil notation "Elliot Cohen Dec. 1947", RG347.7.1, Box 78, folder "AJC Staff Meeting", YIVO. Format modified by present author for presentation.
[205] Mordecai Kosover, "Domestic Implications for a Jewish State," memo, November 17, 1947, *ibid*.
[206] "Minutes of the Meeting of the Committee on Palestine and the AJC Program." January 20, 1948, *ibid*.

> *effectively through the Jewish Community Councils, which are to become centers for Zionist activity in education, relief, combating anti-Semitism and social services.*
>
> *In time, the Jewish Community Councils could become the chief instruments in the great process of making Zionist and Jewish life synonymous throughout the United States.*
>
> *When this aim is achieved, there is no more than one step toward the arising of a central American Jewish body authorized to speak and act in the name of American Jewry.*[207]

As the Israeli State was to be declared, on May 11, 1948 staff met on "Preparation and Distribution of Information on Palestine," plans to "provide a stream of useful material to the communities." The memo says some materials had already been rejected by the AJC "on the ground that some of these items seem too strongly propagandistic, and slanted by the ZOA or other issuing agency." It said the AJC's Department of Public Information

> *will be especially interested in preparation of a fact sheet for columnists, editors and other public media personnel in preparing information of "making the desert bloom" type (Jewish contributions to the Middle East) and other basic information, as well as in current news of a favorable nature, (e.g. a friendly Jewish Palestine as a defense against Communism.)*[208]

A December 1947 memo on "public relations" problems likely to arise from the new state recommended, "We should do everything possible to stress the pioneering and democratic aspects of the new Palestine state."[209]

The memo also recommends that American Jewish leaders be warned,

> *U.S. Jews should not attack the United States Government when it does not side completely with the new Palestinian state on all matters. At least it must be*

---

[207] Mordecai Kosover, "Report on Zionist Thinking and Activities, December 17, 1947, page 3, *ibid.*

[208] "Preparation and Distribution of Information on Palestine," May 12, 1948, *ibid.*

[209] "Preliminary Memorandum on Some of the Public Relations Problems Arising out of Partition of Palestine," page 7, "The Record of the American Jewish Committee in RE Palestine," Vol. 3, AJC.

made clear that whatever objections are raised by Jews to U.S. Government policy are in terms of U.S. interests, or the interests of the UN, rather than in the interests of the new Palestine state.[210]

(Belief in the unseemliness of public schism among the Jewish community was a major motivator of decisions. In February 1944, Undersecretary of State Stettinius in a meeting with AJC staff, "expressed disappointment because the Jews cannot unite. He referred especially to the conflicting views of Judge Proskauer and Stephen Wise and admitted that he was baffled."[211])

---

[210] Page 15, *ibid*.
[211] "Confidential Memorandum MW/JL FEB 1944 ," Box 4.65, file jj-2-104 "Stettinius," JHU.

The Stern Memo: What Kind of State? — 1943

Judge Horace M. Stern* circulated a 1943 essay proposing a coordinated American Jewish approach to Palestine:

> Our principal, indeed our essential requirement is <u>unity</u>...The secret of Anglo-Saxon efficiency is the ability to compromise. If hopelessly discordant views are expressed upon the post-war conference the likely result will be one far less satisfactory to everybody than that which might be accomplished if, by willingness and capacity to make concessions, proposals were unanimously agreed upon and presented on behalf of the Jewish people as a whole.

Stern attempted to bridge the gaps between Zionists and non-Zionist with five propositions that could be agreed upon:

> 1. There is no single solution of the Jewish problem - that is, the problem of providing for the Jewish people assured safety and opportunity for free and happy living. At best, whatever the future of Palestine, the major portion of the Jewish people will have to live in the Diaspora. This makes it correspondingly imperative to obtain protection and guaranties for the Jews in all of the countries of the world...
>
> 2. While Palestine can be a haven for only a part of the Jewish people, its development and welfare are of extreme and urgent importance because of its potentialities as a country in which very large numbers of Jews may dwell under favorable conditions of safety, freedom, and opportunity for full development, and because of the sentimental and emotional urge of large masses of Jews to live in what they regard as the land of their fathers. It is now vital that Zionists and non-Zionists should agree upon a plan, to be submitted to the post-war conference, for the future government of Palestine and for the determination of the status of the Jews with respect to that country. [Stern comments the Arabs will have to accept "an exercise of an international right, analogous to that of eminent domain, with the making of just compensation, for the purpose of providing

---

* Pennyslvania Supreme Court judge and future chief justice; AJC and Jewish Agency member.

shelter for a host of grievously persecuted and homeless people..." Stern intriguingly adds, "Palestine must not be turned into a 'bloody Kansas' through an uncontrolled, hysterical rush there of immigrants. The desirable annual rate of immigration will necessarily depend upon varying economic conditions, although a fixed minimum, substantial in amount, might well be established. That determination should be in the hands of a wholly non-political agency." See Proskauer's 1948 suggestion that Israel limit immigration, page 198.]

3. *Palestine will be of little value to the Jewish people if immigration therein is to be limited to the annual trickle heretofore permitted by England. On the other hand, an unrestrained immigration might plunge the country into economic chaos....There must be established by the United Nations some objective, reasonable standard...*

4. *No country should be compelled to remain forever in tutelage, but, like an individual ward, is entitled to be freed of guardianship...In the case of Palestine, however, it is obvious that if such government were to be established before the Jews are in a majority their continued growth and development there might be imperiled, and the legislation of the country would not be of a nature most conducive to social and economic progress.*

5. *When Palestine is given the right to self-government the government established there must be a democratic, non-sectarian one modeled upon that of the United States, the name and flag of the country to indicate its non-sectarian and democratic character. Palestine shall be "Jewish" only in the sense that the Jewish population, protected by being a majority, will, without fear or hindrance, have the opportunity for free and full development...No laws must be passed giving special rights or privileges of any kind to Jews and distinguished from other citizens. The League of Nations, or whatever similar body may be established after the present war, shall guarantee the observance of the conditions herein set forth.*[212]

---

[212] Horace Stern, unsigned essay on Palestine, with cover letter from Milton E.

A formula for coordination between the AJC and Zionist leaders — support for Jewish settlement in Palestine in exchange for Zionist abjuring of world Jewish nationalism, such as that represented by the World Jewish Congress — was designed in the Weizmann-Stroock conferences of 1941-42.[*]

The AJC agreed to support
> the original purposes of the Balfour declaration whereby there shall be established, for such Jews as now reside there and for such others as choose to go and remain there and for their descendents a legally secured national home in Palestine where they may expect to constitute a majority of the population and may look forward to self government, it being clearly understood that
> a) in such a self-governing community...all the inhabitants...shall enjoy complete equality of rights, and
> b) the establishment of this self-governing community shall in no way affect the political and civil status or allegiance of Jews who are citizens of any other country, no shall any effort at any time be made to effect such status or allegiance and
> c) only such Jews or non-Jews who are or become inhabitants of Palestine may be eligible to become citizens thereof.[213]

In 1942, AJC Executive Committee member James N. Rosenberg angrily objected to the formula for Palestine being developed as a premise for cooperation with the Zionists:

> You set up a kind of democracy which I do not recognize as a democracy; one which begins to work as a democracy only when Jews become a majority there, and only when operating their sole direction, (except perhaps for a sovereign policeman to protect you from

---

Gundersheimer of Associated Jewish Charities of Baltimore to Jacob Blaustein, Oct. 8, 1943. Box 4.65, file JJ-2-98 "Stern, Judge Horace," JHU. Note: present author has extracted from Stern's essay to these numbered points.

[*] A series of conferences begun by Chaim Weizman and then-AJC President Alan M. Stroock. See page 182. The sequence and personalities are described by Morris D. Waldman, executive secretary of the AJC 1929-45, in *Nor By Power*, International Universities Press, New York, 1953.

213 Waldman, *Nor By Power*, pages 229-230.

the surrounding Arab countries). You profess to protect 'equality of rights' for Arabs and Christians though you give them no immigration rights, deny them any part in forming the autonomous commonwealth and demand that Palestine immigration should be conducted to bring about a Jewish majority. Your demand that the exclusive power to set up the 'autonomous commonwealth' be in Jewish hands refutes democracy because it cancels out the rights of others.[214]

Morris Waldman wrote that "we have a fair and reasonable basis for a *modus vivendi* with the Zionists and obtaining from them the very important concession of the eradication of *diaspora* nationalism from Zionism and the attenuation and ultimate cessation of the segregating nationalist propaganda that has worried us."[215]

---

[214] *Nor By Power*, page 232.
[215] *Ibid*, page 250.

"Most of the Yishuv are absolutely blind to any possibility other than Jewish statehood."

A REPORT of September 1947 events from Palestine for the AJC from their regular correspondent Helmut Lowenberg* reported that "There has been quiet in Palestine almost right up to the last few days," when there was a Stern gang bank robbery leaving four British dead, and an Irgun bombing of the Haifa police headquarters killing 10 and injuring 60.[216]

A February 1948 report recounted renewed bloodshed between the British and Jewish terrorists, including unofficial adoption of terrorist tactics by British troops:

> While early in the month relations between the British and the Jews, on the spot here, were just about to improve a trifle, several things happened which caused immense new bitterness on both sides. Early in February, the offices of the "Palestine Post" newspaper in Jerusalem were blown up, and serious damage was done to the paper's staff, office and general workings, It was alleged by the Jewish Agency, on the basis of _prima facie_ evidence, that the explosives had been brought in an army truck which was parked outside the newspaper building shortly before the explosion. Four British policemen were about that time absent from their duties in Jerusalem and were seen fleeing from the scene. Parts of the blown-up truck were later recovered from the wreckage. Combined with the fact that certain British circles here have for the last two years been trying to hinder the appearance of the "Palestine Post" because by its high level of journalism it is an organ critical of and dangerous to British oriental policy and prestige, this has left no Jew here in doubt as to the origin of the attack.
> Again at the end of February an explosion occurred in the main Jerusalem business street which cost over 50 Jewish lives and l50 wounded. This time not one, but 3 trucks of the British army, loaded with explosives, were parked in the road two minutes before the explosion and British soldiers were seen to flee in a Police armoured

---

* A Tel Aviv magistrate and later an Israeli judge.
216"Report from Palestine, Oct. 7, 1947," page 1, ajcarchives.org

> car. A Jewish enquiry committee of well-known and non-political lawyers is sitting to enquire into the explosion. For one who has not seen the evidence it is of course difficult to judge, and in the present time to remain impartial. However, no one, British, Jew or Arab, here really doubts that this outrage was the handiwork of British persons. It appears that the target had been the Histadruth centre in Jerusalem; but there had been an error of judgment.
> A week later, the Stern Gang sought revenge by killing 28 soldiers in a troop train explosion.

Lowenberg seems to attribute bombings by the British to the murky world of "counterinsurgency" operations:

> Of course, nobody here suggested that either the British or the Palestine Government are directly responsible for these two crimes. But, what is clear is that under Police and Army cover, a band of British Fascists "with special methods" of the Farran type is still at large, determined to destroy Jewish lives and property. The responsibility of the Palestine administration consists in ever having allowed such people to become "special anti-terrorist squads" of the security forces, and of still permitting them now to be under army and police cover, even if the "squads" have been disbanded--which is not proved. What is all the more amazing is that in the face of the evidence, and of what is known of Roy Farran[217] and his own police work, the Palestine Government should have seen fit to publish on March 1st a statement of vilification of the Jewish Agency and the whole Yishuv, as a reply to the two bomb attack suspicions.[218]

From the moment of the Nov. 29, 1947 UN General Assembly adoption of the UNSCOP partition plan, it was apparent that it could not peacefully be implemented, in part because Britain would not implement any plan not accepted by all parties, the Arabs of Palestine and the neighboring Arab states were unanimous in rejection of it, and the

---

[217] May 5, 1948 the Rex Farran, the brother of Palestine Government counterinsurgancy police officer Ray Farran was killed by a mail bomb at the family home in Britain, in an attack claimed by Lehi. "Britons Indignant Over Bomb Outrage," New York Times, May 5, 1948, page 17. "British Party Slain," New York Times, May 6, 1948, page 8.

[218] "Report from Palestine, February 1948" page 1-3, "Palestine Correspondent Reports, two reports from AJC's Palestine correspondent (February-March 1948)", ajcarchives.org.

manifest intention of at least the underground armed Jewish groups to establish Jewish control beyond the portion allotted to Jews.

The day before General Assembly vote for Partition, a CIA report flatly stated that as a result of Partition, "armed hostilities between Jews and Arabs will take place."[219]

In February 1948, the CIA reported that Partition "cannot be implemented." If there was a UN reconsideration of its vote for partition, "Jewish violence, however, would undoubtedly continue."[220]

The CIA report recommends the UN Security Council have the "moral courage" to reconsider the plan of Partition. March 19, 1948, US Ambassador Warren Austin told the Security Council that the US would support a Trusteeship as alternative to Partition, perfecting the muddle of American policy in the period leading up to Ben Gurion's declaration of the State of Israel May 14, 1948.[221]

Lowenberg reported from Palestine that the Jews of Palestine were fully consumed by the prospect of statehood, and abashed by the possibility that the United States could back a Trusteeship after having supported Partition.

> *The possibility of a reversal to the federal plan [the 1946 Morrison-Grady plan] arouses curious sentiments among those of the Yishuv whose brain is able to absorb such an idea. The Yishuv as a whole is today more nationalist and more self-confident than ever, as the result of the U.N. partition vote. This means that most of the Yishuv are absolutely blind to any possibility other than Jewish statehood. The very abstract thought of statehood and the decision to bring it about has*

---

[219] "The Consequences of the Partition of Palestine," Nov. 28, 1947, www.foia.cia.gov, page 3.

[220] "Possible Developments in Palestine," Feb. 28, 1948, www.foia.cia.gov, page 1-2.

[221] http://www.trumanlibrary.org/israel/palestin.htm The Security Council members feared the situation was falling to an inevitable doom: "[French representative Alexandre] Parodi observed that even if we are not prepared to do anything, it is very important that we do not give this impression. If we do the Arabs will be hopeless. Even if we have no solution now perhaps we will have in a month or two....I said the situation has obviously been getting worse. We have information that preparations are going on in other countries such as recruiting, financing and the like. Does this mean anything? Is it just a bluff? Should we ignore it? If not, we cannot sit around hoping something will turn up. We will have to make up our minds to do something." "The United States Representative at the United Nations (Austin) to the Secretary of State," March 15, 1948, FRUS, Volume 5, Part II, page 726.

intoxicated Jewish youth. In these circumstances the only thought in the Jewish minds here is of the whole world having to help the Yishuv in realising its particular idea of statehood. The fact that the U.S. and then Russia, should even consider that the present troubles call for a further consideration of the problem by the Big Five, has come as a very big blow. Such a thing was never expected here. This attitude of the nations was decried as lukewarmness or outright betrayal. The intensity of this reaction shows how extreme the Yishuv's public opinion has grown in recent months, and how radical is its nationalism. All this also shows that Agency leadership, which ought to be able to see things in a clearer perspective, is impotent to exert its influence over the Jewish public, except when it leads it in its extremism. All moderating influence seems to have been forfeited.[222]

In view of the obvious relapse of Britain and the U.S. into the arms of the Morrison-Grady Federal Plan, it is questionable whether this proclamation of the Agency will meet with international support. Or whether, on the contrary, it will not be the starting point of friction, diplomatic and otherwise, between the Yishuv and the Anglo-Saxon Front, Many observers here believe that the aim of those who are behind the turn in U.S. policy is to get the Arabs firmly on the Anglo-American side, to put the Jews in the wrong and so to create a hostile front against them. This aim holds immense dangers for the Jews because if the Jews are not careful they might thereby find themselves in the "other camp", that is, in allegiance with the Eastern Bloc. However much the U.S. may in future be opposed, under certain pressure, to the development of Zionism, Jewish leaders will have to beware of a splitting of the Jewish people between the two camps.

The proclamation of the intended establishment of independent Jewish government in May is likely to be strongly opposed by the U.S. and Britain, because...actual Jewish government would be going too far for them. Unless of course the Jews would be content

---

[222]"Report from Palestine, February 1948," page 4-5, "Palestine Correspondent Reports, two reports from AJC's Palestine correspondent (February-March 1948)", ajcarchives.org

to create a Jewish administration subject to some higher authority of a federal or trusteeship government. It may well be that if new U.S. plans are laid open, the Zionists may have to reconsider and limit their intention to that end. At the moment, however, the intention here is to proclaim an autonomous Jewish government on May 16 and not to subject it to any other higher authority, except on terms of complete equality with other member States of the U.N.[223]

The Jews urge for complete political autonomy in their partitioned area. This may lead to clashes with the Anglo-American world, unless they see their way to accepting a compromise formula of "autonomy under the U.N." While neither Palestine Arabs nor Palestine Jews want this civil war, they are not willing to concede to the other's point of view. In the circumstances, the chances of a truce are small. Meanwhile the lamps of civilized orderly government are one by one going out one in this country, and are being replaced in each sector by the candles of autonomy, leaving many dark spots yet to be lighted. The coming month will be one of the most critical in this country's modern history. It will show whether the U.N. and the Jews have been sacrificed to the scare of the third war, or whether there is a vestige of reason and moral[s] left in world politics.[224]

---

[223] Ibid, page 6.
[224] "Report from Palestine, March 1948," page 11.

III. THE AJC AFTER DECLARATION OF THE STATE OF ISRAEL

Commemorative plate produced in Newark, New Jersey, in honor of Israel. Map shows Arab and Jewish areas assigned by the November 29, 1947 United Nations partition plan. Motto is from Theodor Herzl. Darker areas indicate Jewish assigned area, lighter, Arab, with Jerusalem shown white, an international city. (Author photo.) See Jewish settlement areas at time of Partition, page 92.

*The Arabs are incorrigible in never wanting peace — on
the other hand, Israel calls for peace — but its kind.*[225]

Assistant Secretary of State Henry A. Byroade
(1953)

BLAUSTEIN — MAN IN THE CENTER

IN 1939, Jacob — creator, with his father Louis, of the American Oil Company (later AMOCO) — had "relinquished...officerships while retaining his directorships and devoting more time to public affairs"[226] at the age of 47. Since then, he had been building a record of service on US government oil industry boards and in Jewish communal organizations, and in philanthropy and political contributions. Wealth, intelligence, and an energetic and practical manner left him pivotal at the invention of the Zionist state, with excellent entree to the US government.[*]

Jacob was appointed a US delegate to the 10th United Nations General Assembly in 1955. He had been involved with the first meeting of the UN in 1945 in San Francisco. In 1958 he was chairman of the UN's celebration of the tenth anniversary of the Universal Declaration of Human Rights, which he had championed, along with Eleanor Roosevelt.

In his year serving as a UN delegate, he is recorded as arguing unsuccessfully in the US delegation for support of strong UN action against the new South African Apartheid policy.
Mr. Blaustein agreed that we should not retreat on this principle but that on the contrary we should reiterate our support for basic human rights.
The United States abstained on the motion, which failed, which "expressed concern that apartheid was being perpetuated."[227]

---

[225] See page 146.
[226] Letter to Donald Dawson at the White House, April 29, 1952, re: biographical data sent to White House for use announcing appointment of JB to National Advisory Board on Mobilization Policy, Box 2.135, folder q-1-48 "JB VIP Correspondence," JHU.
[*] He also developed close consultations with UN officials, advocated for the Universal Declaration of Human rights, and had comradely relations with Dag Hammarskjöld and Ralph Bunche.
[227] Minutes of the Tenth Meeting of the Delegation to the United Nations General Assembly, New York, October 25,1955," FRUS 1955-1957, Vol. XVIII, page 778.

There were a number of interfaces in which Blaustein was significant:
1. Between American Zionists and non-Zionist American Jews over the creation of a "Jewish" nationality,
2. Between US officials and the newly invented State of Israel, as US foreign policy was to build alliances against the Soviet Union,
3. Between the US State and Defense Departments and the presidency in the Truman and Eisenhower administrations, on issues relating to Israel,
4. Between the American Jewish Committee and the State of Israel.

Blaustein seems to have been a trusted, or at least useful, confidant to many sides, so that (for instance) the President or assistant Secretary of State for Near Eastern affairs could well believe he was a tool to influence Israeli actions for American interests, while the Israeli government fairly could believe he was their advocate in Washington. Blaustein repeatedly said that he felt he was an advocate for Israel within American interests, and Truman and other American officials told him they accepted that description of his position.[228]

Repeatedly, was able to relay to the State Department his understanding of Presidential policy as gained in meetings with Truman, and later Eisenhower, and was able to communicate his standing with them. "JB related the substance of these conferences to Byroade, making clear that the appointment with Dulles was not sought by JB but arranged by the president."[229]

Memos quoted are those prepared by Jacob Blaustein's staff, for his records, unless otherwise noted.

Blaustein's records are voluminous and methodical, and accounts prepared from his memories and notes by his secretary seem reliable and consistent with accounts prepared by his interlocutors. He had close consultations with successive assistant Secretaries of State for Near East Affairs George C. McGhee, Henry A. Byroade, and George V. Allen. Introduction to Blaustein seems to have been part of job orientation for each of these officials:
> *It was good to have had the talk yesterday with Henry Byroade and you and I feel that the same fine relationship in matters of public interest will exist*

---

[228] See exchange with Truman, page 173.
[229] "MEMO Conference Henry A. Byroade with JB (Washington, D.C.) May 23, 1954", item "III - RE JB'S CONFERENCE WITH EISENHOWER AND DULLES," Box 1.73, folder 1460 "AJC Bryoade, General Henry A. 1951-1970," JHU.

between you and me as was always the case with Henry and his predecessor George McGhee.[230]

Blaustein maintained substantive policy consultations with McGhee through the 1960s. Correspondence with Secretaries of State Dean Acheson and John Foster Dulles testify to their interest in having Blaustein coordinate with their staff.

Blaustein's papers show continuous and intimate involvement with both the Israeli and American governments.

With the Israelis, he was involved in detailed consultations on what American officials would be given what posts, and how US policy could be shaped to Israeli needs.[231] (In June 1949, a meeting of leaders of the major Jewish organizations, including Blaustein and Simon Segal of the AJC, was briefed for action by Israeli ambassador to the UN Aubrey S. Eban. The meeting minutes concluded, "It is important that the pro-Arab section of the State Department which again seems to have won the upper hand, Mr. Dean Rusk being the key person in the situation, should be frustrated and that the Jessup formula [to require Israel to cede or pay compensation for land outside that given by the UN partition plan], which only encourages the Arabs in their intransigence, should be abandoned."[232])

Other than an attempt to moderate Israel's claim to be the future home of American Jews, Blaustein immediately in 1948 started to do public policy work for the new state with the Truman administration: loans, *de jure* recognition, arms, resistance to territorial concessions, and establishing as an immutable impossibility the return to their homes of Arab refugees.

To the American government, he propounded that tendencies to extremism in the Israeli government and body politic could be weakened by American support. Arms, money, and advocacy in the United Nations

---

[230] JB to George V. Allen, letter, "Personal," January 26, 1955, Box 1.73, folder 1460 "AJC Byroade, General Henry A. 1951-1970," JHU.

[231] In July 1948, he conferred with Israeli representative Epstein about whether it was more desirable that John H. Hilldring be part of the United States delegation to the United Nations, or have a State Department post. "I was told by some people in Government with whom I discussed it, that they were considering him for the U.N. post and thought he would be able to be more helpful there." "MEMO PHONE COVERSATION, JB to Eliahu Epstein, Minister to [sic] Israel Government in Washington, July 28, 1948," Box 1.48, folder "Eliahu Elath 1948," JHU.

[232] "Memorandum regarding meeting called by Dr. Nahum Goldman[n] of the Jewish Agency to discuss America's recent policy towards Israel ," June 20 1949, ajcarchives.org.

would make Israel more conciliatory to her neighbors. Explicitly, he warned that US condemnation of Israeli policy would "weaken" the reasonable Israeli factions, provoking more likely Israeli military action, and thus complicate peace-making. In 1950,

> JB then urged upon them that it would be most helpful if the United States would do something promptly that would strengthen Weizmann's and Ben Gurion's hands in the election. JB said just as the United States did with the $100,000,000 loan at the time of the first elections in Israel.[233]

In 1954,

> Byroade said... he was realizing that the present policy was bringing about dissension and frustration in Israel and that even though he knew Sharett wanted to keep his people within bounds there might be a possibility that the people there would get out of bounds and even attempt military expansion.....JB said that Byroade was right in his expression that there was an air of frustration being created in Israel...JB said that it was essential that the U.S. do something to correct this and help hold up Sharett's hands.[234]

> ...[On American jet planes and tanks for Israel] *JB said this was very important particularly from the standpoint of Israeli psychology, and also to place them in a better position to defend themselves if the occasion arose.*[235]

Blaustein recorded one achievement:

> *An encouraging thing that JB got out of the conference with Byroade was that he* [Byroade] *is realizing that there is frustration in Israel on account of this American policy* [of what Blaustein called "so-called impartiality"] *and that it is dangerous to have this frustration continue or extend..."*[236]

---

[233] "MEMO JB Conference with McGhee, Berry & Rockwell (Washington), October 17, 1950," page 3, Box 1.56, folder 991 "McGhee Asst. Secretary of State 1949-1950," JHU.
[234] "MEMO Conference Henry A. Byroade with JB (Washington, D.C.), May 24, 1954," Item VI, "RE AMERICAN POLICY," Box 1.73, folder 1460 "AJC Byroade, General Henry A. 1951-1970," JHU.
[235] Item VII, "RE JB's SUGGESTIONS AS TO WHAT MIGHT BE DONE VIS-A-VIS ISRAEL ALONG SECURITY LINES WHICH WOULD IMPROVE THE PSYCHOLOGY OF THE ISRAELIS NOW HAVING FEARS," *ibid.*
[236] Item XI, "A FEW CONCLUSIONS," *ibid.*

Conversely, he repeatedly warned Byroade during the Eisenhower administration that warmer US relations with Arab countries, and an arms deal with Iraq, were counter-productive because the "Arab psychology" would become "intransigent."[237] He previously warned the strategy "might have the effect of causing Sharett to lose control."[238]

After the October 1953 Qibya massacre, "Byroade said [there is] no excuse for what Israel did at Kibya."

> JB said that is the trouble, [the] U.S. has a feeling in order to win Arabs closer to peace, it must lean backwards against Israel and show public signs thereof; that actually U.S. does not seem to understand Arab psychology and that the more the Arabs are kow-towed to, the more intransigent they get and the further removed is peace.*

Blaustein advocated that the United States oppose UN Security Council condemnation of the Qibya massacre, and support instead a more general resolution "denouncing the border incidents." To "avoid recriminations and condemnations," Blaustein "hoped there would be no mention of the Kibya incident." Blaustein said, "if Kibya mentioned at

---

[237] "MEMO Conference Henry A. Byroade with JB (Washington, D.C.) May 24, 1954," Box 1.73, folder 1460 "AJC Byroade, General Henry A. 1951-1970," JHU.

[238] Memo of April 26, 1954 meeting with Byroade, *ibid*:
> JB said that in his view our government should proceed with arms to Iraq only if Iraq agrees to work out an understanding with Israel. Failing to do this, JB said he hopes there will be no implementation of the Iraq Arms Agreement, - but if there is, then the U.S. should do the same for Israel.
> JB said that after all, as he understood it, Israel in 1951 and again in 1952 agreed to accept U.S. arms, meeting all required conditions [of alliance in case of war] - but no arms have been given to Israel.
> Byroade said that as the Israeli Chief of Staff [Moshe Dayan] knows, Israel has more arms than all the other Arab countries put together.
> JB said this is hard to believe and in any event the Arabs seem to have 10 million men they are willing to lose in conflict.
> Byroade said that before the end of the week he hoped to be able to give the green light to Israel for some jet planes requested by Eban.

* The State Department memorandum of the exchange reports, "Nevertheless, Mr. Blaustein was concerned that our arms aid to Iraq, plus the tenor of recent statements by the Administration, were giving rise to a cocksureness and intransigence among the Arab countries. He felt that he knew the Arabs well enough to be sure that you could not afford to give them too much encouragement. Arms to Iraq, he felt sure, would encourage Arab intransigence and it was more likely that these arms would be used against Israel, or even ultimately against the United States, than that they would be used in effective defense against a Soviet threat." "Memorandum of Conversation, by the Director of the Office of Near Eastern Affairs (Hart) SECRET [WASHINGTON,] May 12, 1954," FRUS 1952-1954, Vol. IX, page 1555.

all, there should be mention of the Arab provocations....Byroade said the incursions of individual Arabs to steal, in the course of which they kill individuals is very bad. But not comparable to what Israel did at Kibya."

> Byroade said these incidents set peace back for years. Byroade said [Secretary of State John Foster] *Dulles was surprised and upset that only 4-5 days after Dulles had that friendly, understanding talk with* [Israeli ambassador Abba] *Eban - stating among other things, while Israeli aggression was necessary at the founding of the state, it was not excusable now - which they assume Eban reported back to his country - that 4 or 5 days after <u>that</u> should come the Kibya incident.*

When Jacob asked that a Qibya UN resolution call for negotiations, an exasperated Byroade told Jacob "he knows the Arabs are incorrigible in never wanting peace -- on the other hand, Israel calls for peace -- but its kind."[239]

In a perfect symmetry in the exchanges, Blaustein promoted twin concepts that "Israeli psychology" would be improved by support and arms, and "Arab psychology" by strategic distance.

The AJC under his presidency framed support for the new State as meeting a Cold War challenge of preventing reliance of Israel on the eastern (Communist) block, and as finding in Israel a providentially placed US ally. (This succeeded the original British intention of the Jewish homeland in Palestine as a forward base of British Empire.[240])

One of his most effective strategies seems to have been the promotion of Israel as a US Cold War military asset.[241] After one visit to Israel in 1950, conferring with Ben Gurion and other leaders, Blaustein told US officials "he was assured that Israel can be counted on 100% as an ally of

---

[239] "MEMO Conference Assistant Secretary of State for Near Eastern, South Asian and African Affairs, Henry A. Byroade (Washington) and JB (Byroade's Office), October 29, 1953," Box 1.73, folder 1460 "AJC Byroade, General Henry A. 1951-1970," JHU.
[240] See page 105.
[241] "Mr Blaustein stated that it might be advisable for Israel to give officially some real evidence of its Western orientation...some further steps might be taken which would indicate not only to the high government officials but also to the people of the United States that Israel can be counted upon; indeed, one of the arguments that Mr. Blaustein used during his discussions with the President, Secretary of Defense, [Louis] Johnson and the Secretary of State, [Dean] Acheson and Mr. McGee(sic) in favor of providing arms for Israel...was that Israel is a bastion of democracy in the Middle East." "Meeting with Mr. Ben-Gurion," August 13, 1950, page 5, Box 3.6, folder "Ben Gurion Talks & Public Relations 1950 1 of 2," JHU.

the United States, both politically and militarily...that in the event of world conflict the only allies the United States would have in the Near East who could really help are Israel and Turkey."[242] In 1952, he argued the Israeli need for more arms, while "Byroade said that Israel already has arms way beyond that which the other countries have."[243]

With Truman and with McGhee, he propounded that maximum Jewish immigration to Israel fed Israel's military manpower, which would have it more able to fight with the USA any future war against the Soviets.[244] This policy of maximal immigration increased Israel's need for territory, and made impossible any return of Arab refugees.[245] (The ideological character of Israel as an open home for future Jewish *olim* makes establishing border limits problematic still.)

He consistently propounded the principle that arms given to Arab countries should be accompanied by strengthening Israel. Discussing an upcoming meeting McGhee was to have with the Egyptian foreign minister, "JB went on to caution that he did not think the United States should send arms to Egypt unless Israel got them correspondingly."[246]

A Baltimore-born American, having built with his father an iconic American enterprise, AMOCO, he created a formula — the Ben Gurion-Blaustein Exchange of 1950 — to serve as a protective wall against the ambiguity of American Jewish "dual loyalty." That provided an authoritative rationale which allowed active support by American Jews of the Israeli government.[247]

In 1951, Jacob's significant enmeshment among the players in United States policy to Israel can be read in this memo from McGhee to Secretary Acheson:

> On July 5, Jacob Blaustein, President of the American Jewish Committee and a prominent oil man, told me he did not think that the Mutual Security Program provided

---

[242] "MEMO JB Conference with McGhee, Berry & Rockwell (Washington), October 17, 1950," page 2, Box 1.56, folder 991 "McGhee Asst. Secretary of State 1949-1950," JHU.
[243] "MEMO JB Conference with Henry A. Byroade, Ass't Sec. of State (Washington), October 9, 1952," Item III, "Middle East - Israel," Box 1.73, folder 1460 "AJC Byroade, General Henry A. 1951-1970," JHU.
[244] See page 174 and 199.
[245] See page 195 *et seq.*
[246] "MEMO JB Conference with McGhee... October 17, 1950," page 6-7.
[247] "This is Israel's clarification of the fact that we Americans have always regarded as axiomatic - that the allegiance of American Jews is to America alone," JB to George C. McGhee, letter, October 18, 1950, Box 1.56, folder 991 "McGhee Asst. Secretary of State 1949-1950," JHU.

sufficient economic assistance for Israel. ...and suggested that the allocations for Israel and the Arab states be raised from $23.5 million to $75 million apiece. He said that if this were possible, he was sure he could get Congressional leaders to withdraw their bills for $150 million[for Israel].[248]

---

[248] "Memorandum by the Assistant Secretary of State for Near Eastern, South Asian, and African Affairs (McGhee) to the Secretary of State [WASHINGTON,] July 17, 1951," FRUS 1951, Vol. V, page 775.

Advocacy for the New State

AFTER THE war that followed partition and the declaration of the State of Israel, Blaustein and other Jewish leaders were significant participants in the 1948 re-election campaign of President Harry S. Truman. Jacob had been a frequent visitor to the White House, and was active in the Democratic National Finance Committee.

While in the February 1948 speech in Baltimore Blaustein referred to the "extreme, political Zionists" of the Biltmore declaration,[249] later in the same year the AJC was working in American politics to obtain for the state declared by those "extremists" arms and recognition, to protect their conquests of land, and to ensure the Arab refugees from those lands could not return home.

The papers of Jacob Blaustein are rich with records of phone calls and visits with President Truman, both as an officer of the AJC and as a significant figure in the oil industry, and with press clippings recording the contacts, such as "Jacob Blaustein Calls on Truman" in December 1948:

> *Washington, Dec. 20 — Jacob Blaustein, of Baltimore, president of the American Oil Company, today discussed with President Truman the relationships between business and Government.*
> *Blaustein spent fifteen minutes with the President....The President, he added, had been very understanding of the industry's problems....*[250]

Blaustein's memo of that Dec. 20, 1948 meeting with President Truman records that the meeting lasted more than 35 minutes. Besides discussing a proposed federal "excess profits tax" and tidelands oil drilling, "JB told the President that he hoped he would see to it so that in the future the State Department did not sabotage his wishes[regarding Palestine policy]. The president said that after much difficulty he had gotten the Palestine situation on track and he proposed to keep it there - and to leave the State Department to him. JB said that he would like to suggest, particularly since Israeli's (sic) admission to the UN had been delayed that early *de jure* recognition by the U.S. is essential. The President said that he proposed that that be done as soon as the January

---

249 Page 23.
250 Baltimore Evening Sun, Dec. 20, 1948, clipping in Box 2.21, file C-2-70 "Truman, Harry - Campaign 1948," JHU.

Israeli elections are over. JB said he assumed that the matter of the U.S. Loan for Israel is progressing satisfactorily and the President said it is."[251]

Blaustein told the President that he looked forward to being a liaison to American Jewish organizations, and "The President said that he also had the highest regard for the American Jewish Committee and as a matter of fact it was the only Jewish organization with whom he felt he could really work."

In a conversation with Jacob the day following the re-election of Truman November 2, 1948, AJC executive vice president John Slawson exclaimed that "it is a definite refutation of the reactionary tendency toward which we were going such as the committee on [Un-]American activities" and expressing certainty that "We are going to get a DP [immigration] bill; we're going to get everything..."[252]

The same day, Blaustein solicitously called the assistant to the Democratic Party's finance chairman to enquire, "What is the situation on money? Have they got all they need? Or, will they have a deficit they got to make up?"[253]

In July 1948, Blaustein wrote Proskauer,
Shertok's [Sharett's] aims in his cable to you are definitively included in the Democratic platform. I had something to do with that in Philadelphia. This, of course, may mean little with the uncertainties of the election, but maybe Truman can be induced to translate these points into action before election. Shall we try?[254]

Secretary of Defense James V. Forrestal's diaries describe his failed behind-the-scenes efforts to have the Truman and Thomas E. Dewey campaigns agree to declare the Palestine issue "off-limits" to US electoral politics.

The 1948 Democratic Party Platform on Israel was detailed in its support for Israeli aims:

---

[251] "MEMO JB Conference with President Truman, December 20, 1948," Box 2.115, folder N-5-65, "Truman, Harry S.," JHU.
[252] November 3, 1948 phone transcript, "JB to John Slawson and Miss Kushell, NY," Box 2.21, file C-2-70 "Truman, Harry - Campaign 1948", JHU.
[253] Nov. 3, 1948 phone transcript, "JB TO MAY OLIVER," *ibid.*
[254] Blaustein to Proskauer, July 12, 1948, page 2, Box 2.21, file C-2-23 "Proskauer, Judge Joseph M.," JHU. July 28, 1948, Blaustein reported to Israeli representative Eliahu Epstein that "I worked hard at the convention" for the Democratic Palestine platform plank. Handwritten notes of conversation, Box 1.48, folder "Eliahu Elath 1948," JHU.

> *President Truman, by granting immediate recognition to Israel, led the world in extending friendship and welcome to a people who have long sought and justly deserve freedom and independence.*
> *We pledge full recognition to the State of Israel. We affirm our pride that the United States under the leadership of President Truman played a leading role in the adoption of the resolution of November 29, 1947, by the United Nations General Assembly for the creation of a Jewish State.*
> *We approve the claims of the State of Israel to the boundaries set forth in the United Nations resolution of November 29th and consider that modifications thereof should be made only if fully acceptable to the State of Israel.*
> *We look forward to the admission of the State of Israel to the United Nations and its full participation in the international community of nations. We pledge appropriate aid to the State of Israel in developing its economy and resources.*
> *We favor the revision of the arms embargo to accord to the State of Israel the right of self-defense. We pledge ourselves to work for the modification of any resolution of the United Nations to the extent that it may prevent any such revision.*
> *We continue to support, within the framework of the United Nations, the internationalization of Jerusalem and the protection of the Holy Places in Palestine.*[255]

The 1948 Republican Platform was also fulsome, but less detailed:
> *We welcome Israel into the family of nations and take pride in the fact that the Republican Party was the first to call for the establishment of a free and independent Jewish Commonwealth. The vacillation of the Democrat Administration on this question has undermined the prestige of the United Nations. Subject to the letter and spirit of the United Nations Charter, we pledge to Israel full recognition, with its boundaries as sanctioned by the United Nations and aid in developing its economy.*[256]

---

[255] http://www.presidency.ucsb.edu/ws/index.php?pid=29599
[256] http://www.presidency.ucsb.edu/ws/index.php?pid=25836. AJC Foreign Affairs director Simon Segal was asked to draft a "proposed plank" for the Republican platform, for use by George Mintzer. "Memo to John Slawson, AJC Executive Vice President, regarding the proposed Palestine plank for the Republican National

In Blaustein's phone transcripts with other fund-raisers during the campaign, there is discussion of what is desired from the Truman administration, including *de jure* recognition of the State of Israel, loans, and administration support for Israel to resist unwelcome boundary changes to make an armistice. The day before his Sept. 17, 1948 assassination in Jerusalem by the Jewish terrorist group Lehi ("Stern Gang"), UN Security Council Palestine mediator Count Folke Bernadotte had proposed a plan that had the Israeli forces withdrawing from some territories they had captured, "inclusion of the whole or part if the Negeb in Arab territory," and the return of Arab war refugees.[257]

A September 17 letter from Blaustein to Proskauer reiterates the requests that were being made to Truman:

> *I was asked to the White House twice within the past week in connection with matters other than those of direct concern to the American Jewish Committee. Yesterday, however, when I had more than a half hour with the President alone, I urged that some positive things be done promptly with respect to Palestine, primarily because they are just and proper, and necessary to further and insure peace and order. I pointed out that more is required than just the de facto recognition and the appointment of the Minister to Israel.*
> *I specified de jure recognition, not delaying same until after the Israeli elections, an early loan, appointment of General Hilldring to the State Department (which James McDonald deems essential), urging the Arabs to negotiate peace directly with the Jews, and backing UN recognition of Israel when application is made.*
> *The President was very sympathetic and when I left him I believed there was a good chance of something being done with respect to some of these items, especially the loan and Hilldring and maybe de jure recognition.*
> *Today, however, I do not know what adverse effect*

Convention," June 4, 1948, ajcarchives.org.

[257] Bernadotte reported to the UN on September 16, 1948, "It would be an offence against the principles of elemental justice if these innocent victims of the conflict were denied the right to return to their homes while Jewish immigrants flow into Palestine, and, indeed, at least offer the threat of permanent replacement of the Arab refugees who have been rooted in the land for centuries. ...As a result of the conflict in Palestine, almost the whole of the Arab population fled or was expelled from the area under Jewish occupation." "Progress Report of the United Nations Mediator on Palestine," http://unispal.un.org/UNISPAL.NSF/0/AB14D4AAFC4E1BB985256204004F55FA

Bernadotte's murder may have.[258]

In this exchange, Dewey Stone of Boston raises the idea that future Jewish financial support for campaigns be tied to satisfactory fulfillment of Israeli aims for US policy:

Dewey Stone [of Boston]: And I'll tell you what I think we ought to do… [ellipses original] I talked with Greenfield from Philadelphia. Now I feel as though they [Truman campaign] are definitely putting the "heat" on us and getting much more money from us than they are morally entitled to, considering what they themselves are doing and considering what they're not doing for us and I think as a matter of practical politics, as well as morality, that we ought to begin to check with each other and hold back. Now, I gave them five for myself and I gave them an extra five from a couple of my friends the other day.

JB: Uh-huh.

S: And Greenfield is giving them fifty; you've given them money; Ed Klinberg gave them seventy-five that he got from our group. Ed Kauffman has picked up pretty close to fifty that he got from some of my friends and his and I talked with Jim Brown--- I mean Charlie Brown in Los Angeles and with Ben Swig in San Francisco and with Rudolph up in Syracuse and the fellow up in Albany and a friend of mine in Chicago and as near as I can pick up the figures, they're getting about 65 to 70 per cent of their money from our people. I think we ought to stop giving them another damn dime until they do something.

JB: The difficulty is, of course, there isn't much time left to do anything and what we want is not a mere statement though. I heard that when he talks in New York, he may say something, but that isn't what we want.

S: We prepared and actually wrote out word for word, the text of de jure recognition which is a very simple statement of facts. Then we prepared a press release for him to issue in conjunction with it, in which he would say that he reaffirms the Democratic platform but there

---

[258] "Jacob Blaustein to John Slawson, AJC executive vice president, regarding meeting with President Harry Truman, " September 17, 1948, ajcarchives.org. Letter to Proskauer is attached.

> would be no boundary changes made in the State of
> Israel, without the <u>consent</u> of the State of Israel.
> (Indistinct) he did not order import, export men to make
> a loan, but he is urging them to expedite it. Now, we went
> into it. We had Bob Nathan there; we had Oscar Gantz;
> we had Ginsberg. Joe Keenan was there representing
> them and one other fellow and there was Ed Kauffmann.
> There was Judge Lebenthal; there was Greenfield who is
> very close to them, from Philadelphia.

After discussing Truman not over-ruling Secretary of State George C. Marshall as they wished:

> JB: In any event, it certainly seems that if there is a right in the thing, that the top ought to insist on that right.
>
> S: As long as we continue to accept the morality of his dilly-dallying by doing almost as much as we would do if he did everything we want, we are losing a very..... [ellipses in original]
>
> JB: Yeah. I agree with you. I agree with you.
>
> S: That was the thing I wanted to discuss with you....I am amazed to find the number of them that already kicked in very substantially and you heard the total amount of money they raised and when I see how much of it we've given and after all, we're only four or five per cent of the people, there is a limit to the extent to which we ought to lend ourselves to being used.
>
> JB: Yeah. Yeah. All right. We're in agreement. Now look, if you learn anything further I ought to know, let me know and if I learn anything, I'll let you know.[259]

A few days later,

> JB: Well, I'm for him for a number of reasons. I'm for him because I feel that the liberal things I've been standing and devoting a lot of my life to, are in better hands with the Democratic Administration than with reactionary groups.
>
> G[Albert M. Greenfield]: Indeed, you're right. We're for him on that basis and we check on that basis too. I mean, we're in accord fairly. Now on the very important

---

[259] October 22, 1948 phone transcript, Blaustein to Dewey Stone, JHU Box 2.21 C-2-70 "Truman, Harry - Campaign 1948"

question, the foreign question which is very close to my heart, as a Jew, I must say that he's already done as much, if not more than all of his predecessors put together.

JB: Well, we're in agreement about the individual and we're in agreement that we've <u>got</u> to do whatever we can. I understand that some of our friends are very disappointed.

G: Well, they ought not to be if you're talking about Dewey Stone.

JB: Yeah.

G: I think I straightened him out with Lou Lebenthal's help, a few moments ago. I really think that we was going too strong and he might have done some harm, more to himself than anybody else, in his demands. You follow me?

JB: Yeah. Yeah.

G: We should not be given to looking a gift horse in the mouth.

JB: No, but it is a fact. I mean, not as a reason now for not trying to do everything we can because I think it will be very unfortunate, even if he doesn't win and even if there isn't a Democratic majority in the Senate, there will be a large group there and Howard will be in there and I hate like the devil to have the record finally show that so many of our people ran out. I mean on the contribution side. I'm agreeing with you all the way down the line.

G: I'm glad to hear you say that. There ought to be no ingratitude.

JB: The other side of it is, I can see how people might feel that this thing not only is untimely, but isn't sufficient and yet it is probably the best he could do with that other fellow at the head of the department. [Marshall] That's his problem.[260]

On Nov. 16, 1948 Stone wrote Blaustein,

---

[260] October 25, 1948 phone transcript, Albert Greenfield to JB, pg 4-5, Box 2.21 C-2-70 "Truman, Harry - Campaign 1948," JHU.

> *I know you feel, as I do, that he [Truman] will honestly and sincerely and as soon as possible, fulfill all of his promises to us.*
>
> *I am trying to make as accurate an appraisal as possible of the financial assistance he received from our group and at your convenience I will appreciate either a call or a memo from you, telling me what you were able to directly and indirectly accomplish for them.*[261]

The 1948 campaign file in Blaustein's papers has hundreds of items, before and after the election. There are telegrams from campaign fundraiser Louis A. Johnson[*] to Jacob to raise money for radio, newspaper ads, travel, and then to retire the campaign deficit, and thank you notes from Harry Truman, like this April 1, 1949 note on White House stationary:

> *Dear Mr. Blaustein:*
> *Nat Lichtblau has told me of his conversation with you of a few days ago.*
> *I just want to express my thanks and tell you how happy I am to know that we can*
> *count on your help.*
> *Very sincerely yours,*
> *[signed] Harry Truman*[262]

Lichtblau was listed by *Time* magazine, along with Blaustein, as one of the "angels" of the 1948 Truman campaign: "Nathan Lichtblau, 45, Manhattan plastics manufacturer... served as Johnson's deputy, wheedled many a sweat-stained dollar from New York's minority groups when the going was tough."[263]

Time's entry for Blaustein read: "Jacob Blaustein, 56, a multimillionaire who lives at Pikesville, Md. Blaustein built a fortune in Texas and Pan American oil, is now president of the American Trading & Production Corp. A friend of Franklin Roosevelt, he made surveys of D.P.s in Germany, was vice-chairman of the Petroleum Administration for War Marketing Committee. He is now president of the American Jewish Committee. Vice President Barkley attended a testimonial dinner

---

261 Letter from Dewey D. Stone, *ibid.*
* Secretary of Defense 1949-50.
262 Truman to Blaustein, April 1, 1949, Box 2.21, C-2-70 "Truman, Harry - Campaign 1948," JHU.
263 "The Angels of the Truman Campaign," *Time*, June 6, 1949.

this month for Blaustein, for 'his untiring efforts in behalf of world Jewry.'"

Two days after Truman's election victory, Blaustein asked Lichtblau, "[Louis] Johnson and those fellows feel I did my part, don't they?"

"You are one of the two or three that we do feel that way about," Lichtblau replied. "I want them to feel that," Blaustein said.[264]

Drawing a distinction between Zionist groups he felt had been hectoring him and the AJC, February 12, 1949 Truman wrote Blaustein in reply to Blaustein's February 2 thank-you letter for *de jure* recognition and a loan for Israel, "I became thoroughly disgusted with some of the high pressure groups during the difficult times through which we had to go from 1946 to date..."[265]

The American Jewish Committee was determined to be seen as influential by its members, and to avoid an "ineffective position" with the new state of Israel.[266] With his February 2 letter, Blaustein attached a note to presidential secretary Matthew J. Connelly, objecting that the American Jewish Committee had not been included in the ceremony marking recognition of Israel by the United States:

> *Between us, if I may say so, we cannot help but wonder why, after all the constructive work the American Jewish Committee has done with regard to the solution in Palestine in a manner which the President has approved, added to my personal support of the President throughout - we were neglected in the ceremony and pens in connection with the de jure recognition of Israel.*
>
> *I am getting this off my chest to you personally because situations like this affect the acceptance of organizations by their constituencies and this ommission(sic) may impair our effectiveness in this field.*
[267]

---

[264]"November 4, 1948 MEMO / PHONE CONVERSATION Nat Lichtblau, New York, to JB," *ibid.*
[265]Harry S. Truman to Jacob Blaustein, February 12, 1949, Box 1.30 folder 416 "AJC - Truman, President," JHU.
[266]See page 181.
[267]Jacob Blaustein to Matthew J. Connelly, February 2, 1949, small typewritten note attached to letter to President Truman, *ibid.*

"Not only her own interests are involved, but those of the Jews in the United States and all over the world."

In July 1949, when the "AJC Policy and Israel" committee met on the problem of treatment of Christian and Catholic people and holy places in the new state — and unresponsiveness of Israeli officials to complaints and requests for information — the perceived danger to Jews elsewhere from Israeli actions was spelled out, and a pragmatic argument to present to Israel to not damage its most important assets:

> *Elliot E. Cohen was of the opinion that this memorandum* [to foreign minister Sharett] *has to emphasize before the Israeli Government that our own strength here*[Jews in the US], *as well as of Jewish communities abroad, is of great importance to Israel....*
> *Although Israel is interested in a political victory on all fronts, it should be emphasized to her government as strongly as possible that not only her own interests are involved, but those of the Jews in the United States and all over the world. Israel will therefore have to listen to our requests and suggestions.*[268]

In March 1950, Simon Segal told the AJC "Committee on the Impact of Israel" that AJC policy was to thread the area between Zionist doctrine and the anti-Jewish state American Council for Judaism:

> *The AJC is frequently on tenterhooks to counteract the unguarded remarks of Ben-Gurion or quick to challenge the Council for Judaism on its right to air its views in the public press...What is required is a more realistic attitude toward Israel, an attitude which will not blindly support it, particularly when Israel diverges from our views, whether in the area of human rights or in matters before the United Nations. In regard to the Council, a more incisive approach is required, an approach which will enunciate clearly our differences with them....Mr. [Louis] BREIER ... taxed the AJC with avoiding a major task, that is, the spelling out of the exact content of our beliefs, while assaulting the Council or Zionists for theirs. What specifically is our conception of being a Jew? The Council*

---

[268] "MINUTES A meeting of the Committee on Israel and AJC Policy was held on Monday, July 11, 1949 at 4:00 P.M. in the Conference Room," in "AJC Committees on Israel File, Foreign Affairs Department, FAD-1. Memoranda on relationship of American Jews to Israel, 1951-1955," ajcarchives.org

at least presents a consistent view in predicating religion as the sole link among Jews.

The committee formulated "tentative postulates" of its position:

1. *It is possible and desirable to have Jewish communities in any part of the democratic world.*
2. *There exists a Jewish community, in a real sense, apart and beyond the mere aggregation of Jewish individuals.*
3. *There is a sentiment of kinship, mutual responsibility and solidarity, among the Jewish communities throughout the world.*
4. *The Jews, in their history, have crystallized certain traditional convictions and aspirations about the relation of individual to individual and individual to society.*[269]

In April 1950, the AJC "Impact of Israel" committee examined the emerging meanings of the support the American Jewish community was giving, in fact, to the Israeli state:

Mr. [Morroe] Berger argued that, in view of the close relation between the State of Israel and the Jewish community in Israel and considering the fact that the fate of the community depends to a great degree upon the fate of its political expression, it is artificial to speak of support for the one and to ignore the other. The more schools and hospitals we support, for example, the more arms the State can afford to buy. No one, he continued, will be convinced or fooled by this distinction. ...in Israel, helping the Jewish community in almost any way means helping the state meet the normal and growing responsibilities of a modern democratic state to the community. We ought to recognize these facts explicitly, Mr. Berger concluded, and assert that American Jewry wants, and properly so, to see a flourishing and strong State of Israel.

Dr. [Simon] Segal disputed this position, pointing out that a state is an abstraction, not an end in itself. We want, rather, to help people, not a political abstraction. But, he continued, he would raise another question: in

---

[269] "IMPACT OF ISRAEL COMMITTEE MEETING, Thursday March 16, 1950, Grammercy [sic] Park Hotel - New York City, MINUTES," *ibid.*

view of the fact that American Jews as a whole would consider Israel's failure (that is, its weakness, attack upon it and military defeat) a catastrophe, do we therefore want to help build up the power of Israel to prevent such a fate?

Most of the members of the Committee felt that American Jews, and they themselves, would in fact consider such failure a catastrophe because it would 1) lay Jews open to the charge that they cannot ever maintain their own state and community, 2) reduce Jewish prestige enormously, and 3) stimulate or increase insecurity among world and certainly American Jewry.

If we agree that we want to strengthen Israel, Dr. [S. Andhil] Fineberg said, just where do we stop? There must be a "ceiling" to our support for and identification with Israel.

A discussion of this question led to agreement by most of those present that <u>it is desirable that American Jewry not only extend aid but also consciously try to influence Israel to progress further and further in a democratic way</u>. It was agreed that it is wise and proper for American Jews to offer American democracy as a model for Israel.
...As to Ben-Gurion's statements and the halutz[pioneer] movement in the U.S., the Committee favored, not counter-propaganda in a narrow sense, but a positive program which would stress the security of American Jews and would promote Jewish values here.[270]

---

[270] "Minutes of the Second Meeting of the Committee on the Impact of Israel Monday, April 10, 1950," *ibid.*

Qibya, 1953: "Adds one more ugly feature to an image already displeasing to many Americans."

In October 1953, the State of Israel launched a "retaliatory" raid on a West Bank village, by a commando force ("Force 101") led by young Ariel Sharon, leading to worldwide condemnation. The UN armistice commission reported:

> The crossing of the demarcation line by a force approximating one half of a battalion from the Israel regular army, fully equipped, into Qibya village on the night of 14-15 October 1953 to attack the inhabitants by firing from automatic weapons and throwing grenades and using bangalore torpedoes together with TNT explosive, by which forty-one dwelling houses and a school building were completely blown up, resulting in the cold-blooded murder of forty-two lives, inc1uding men, women [and] children, and the wounding of fifteen persons and the damage of a police car, [and] at the same time, the crossing of a part of the same group into Shuqba village, [are] a breach of article III, paragraph 2 of the General Armistice Agreement.[271]

This action, commonly called the Qibya Massacre, compounded a previous crisis in which the UN Security Council condemned Israel, and the Eisenhower administration cut off US aid to Israel, for refusing UN orders to stop construction work to divert waters of the Jordan River at B'not Yaakov.

October 21, 1953, Ambassador Eban passed the false Israeli denial of responsibility for the raid to AJC foreign affairs director Simon Segal, claiming that because of border incidents,

> the Israeli government has provided arms and equipment to the border settlements which are composed mostly of recent immigrants for their self-defense. It is the people of these settlements who have retaliated against the infiltration from Jordan including the recent retaliatory action in Kibya.[272]

---

[271] UN Security Council Records, Eighth Year, 635th Meeting, 9 November, 1953, page 8.
[272] Simon Segal to Dr. John Slawson, memo, October 21, 1953, "Subject: Meeting with Ambassador Eban, Israel Consulate, October 20th, 4:00 p.m.," page 2. "Israel, Foreign Affairs Department Collection, FAD. Reports on American Jews and Israel, the American Council for Judaism, and a meeting with Israeli Ambassador Abba Eban, October 1953," ajcarchives.org

The AJC did make a public condemnatory statement of the Israeli raid on Oct. 26: "Repeated attacks on Israeli settlements may explain the Kibya incident, but cannot justify it. Violence and bloodshed should be condemned, whether by Arabs or Israelis."[273] [274]

Even before the crisis of the Qibya raid, the AJC had been examining the challenges the new State of Israel presented to the place of Jews in America, as in the discussions in the previous chapter.

On October 5, 1953, in a document titled, "AMERICAN JEWS AND ISRAEL: Questions Affecting the Views of the American Jewish Committee Today," the AJC examined issues that had been simmering:
> Today, American citizens are speaking up for Israel. On such issues as Arab refugees or the nationalization of Jerusalem, most American Jews rally to Israel's side. How should we regard this spontaneous identification? Is it desirable that Jews in the USA should stake their status on the necessarily unpredictable policies of a government which is not their own?...
>
> 1. What constitutes proper AJC assistance to Israel?
> 2. What attitudes toward Israel should we encourage among American Jews?
> 3. What efforts, if any, should we make to influence United States policy and public opinion concerning Israel?
> 4. What demands may we justifiably make on Israel?

Again[*], there was the issue that aid to Jews in Palestine — aid that before the Israeli state was declared was considered philanthropic — had become military aid to a State of Israel at war:
> AID TO ISRAEL -- WHERE DO WE DRAW THE LINE?
> In considering to what degree AJC -- or American Jews in general -- should help Israel, the existence of a political entity in that land is a complicating factor.

---

[273]*In Vigilant Brotherhood*, AJC, 1964, page 37. Also, a November 7, 1953 press release quotes it, in "American Jews & Israel File, Foreign Affairs Department Collection, FAD-1. Memoranda on Relationship of American Jews to Israel, 1951-1955," ajcarchives.org.

[274]"Following the deplorable Kibya attack, our Executive Committee last October forthrightly condemned acts of violence that had been committed by *both* sides." "HIGHLIGHTS OF 1953," by Irving M. Engel, Chairman, Executive Committee, AJC, *American Jewish Year Book*, Vol. 56 (1955), page 631.

[*] See page 159.

> Many years before the new state came into being, donations for relief, social welfare, education and culture flowed from America to Palestine. Such funds, still going abroad on a substantial scale, are traditionally approved as philanthropic contributions, in contrast to financial aid for military needs, which would be frowned upon.
> But is the distinction real?
> It stands to reason that, the more Israel is helped to multiply her population, the more her military reserves expand. Philanthropic contributions for immigrant relief ease the governments financial burden and free additional funds for defense. Thus, American dollars sent and spent in good faith for relief in Israel can nevertheless be said to further the military program of a foreign state.
> The American Jewish Committee does not give money to Israel or raise money for it. However, our representatives [AJC President Blaustein and others] played a major part in the negotiations leading to the [reparations] agreement with West Germany, whereby Israel will receive about three-quarters of a billion dollars.[275]

The memo postulated that American public opinion of Israel would affect gentile views of Jews.

> It goes without saying that whatever moves we make to influence government policy must frequently be buttressed by appeals to public opinion.
> But in the case of Israel, American public opinion must be cultivated for other reasons as well -- notably for our own self-interest.
> The experience of other religious groups leads us to believe that like or dislike for Israel may cause like or dislike for American Jews....
> Just as 19th century attitudes toward Catholics in Britain were colored by happenings in Italy and Spain, so it is likely that attitudes toward Jews in America are now being colored by what happens in Israel.
> This being so, American Jews want to make sure that their Christian neighbors know about the favorable

---

[275] "AMERICAN JEWS AND ISRAEL: Questions Affecting the Views of the American Jewish Committee Today," October 5, 1953, Page 2, "Record of the American Jewish Committee in RE Palestine," Vol 4, AJC.

> aspects of Israeli life. We are anxious to publicize the heroism of Israelis for the same reason that we promote knowledge of American war heroes who are Jewish.
> Considering, however, our apprehension concerning too close association in the public mind between American Jews and Israel, the public relations profits gained by advertising Israeli virtues may actually reinforce an identification which we are trying to break down.
> In the case of Israel, there is an additional danger: we may praise its democracy today; but tomorrow Mapam [party], with its pro-Soviet orientation, may come to power in the government. And even now there are such regrettable realities as the discriminatory features of the Israeli nationality law, the land acquisition law, and the clerical monopoly of legal power over marriage and divorce.[276]

The Qibya public relations crisis seems to have tipped the balance for a decision by the AJC that working for the public image of Israel in the United States was an imperative for the status and security of American Jews, lest Israel fall into disfavor with non-Jewish Americans, and American Jews along with her.

A weight to the decision may have been an October 20 meeting with Ambassador Eban:
> Eban told Segal that the American administration had been exhibiting a pattern of being too sympathetic to Arab positions, including on the Jordan river diversion project and the Quibya raid.
> In the discussion views were expressed that the problem of the recent incidents should be placed in the context of the entire security problem in the Near East. Also it was felt that there is great need for immediate action on the part of the Jewish community and other friends of Israel in the U.S. to reverse the trend that seems to be prevalent now in the State Department. Of course it was decided that this cannot be discussed with the ambassador or representatives of Israel but that this is an American problem and must be considered by American Jews alone. How such action should be organized and what the strategy ought to be was

---

276 Page 8, *ibid*.

therefore left for future consideration by American Jewish organizations.[277]

Six days later, October 27, an AJC document titled "Public Relations Factors in the Israel Situation" observed the Qibya raid was not an isolated public relations problem for Israel in America:

The border incidents, while recently claiming most attention in the press, must not be regarded as dominant factors. We must also take into account longstanding issues which have been interpreted to the marked disadvantage of Jews.

For example, in debates on the internationalization of Jerusalem, Jews have been pictured as callous to the most sacred claims and concerns of other religions; the problem of Arab refugees has been posed as an outcome of Jewish inhumanity and ruthlessness; and the Jordan River Water Project has been cited as an example of Jewish rapaciousness.

Thus, the Kibya incident, wherein Jews appear as cold-blooded killers of women and children, adds one more ugly feature to an image already displeasing to many Americans.

In other words, this is not just a crisis situation brought on by events of the past two weeks. We have here a problem that has been in the making for some time past and which calls for remedial action on more than one count.

The document foresaw consequences dangerous to American Jews of a change in US public opinion:

Attitude of American public opinion toward Israel.
1. The reservoir of goodwill which Israel has enjoyed in this country may be drained. In this event, there is bound to be a stiffening on the part of the State Department and the Administration generally toward Israel's demands. This in turn will react unfavorably on American public opinion.
2. If the American people and government turn against Israel, the hand of the Mapam(Communist Party of

---

[277] Simon Segal to Dr. John Slawson, memo, October 21, 1953, "Subject: Meeting with Ambassador Eban, Israel Consulate, October 20th, 4:00 p.m.," page 4. "Israel, Foreign Affairs Department Collection, FAD. Reports on American Jews and Israel, the American Council for Judaism, and a meeting with Israeli Ambassador Abba Eban, October 1953. (5)(October 1953)," ajcarchives.org.

Israel) may be strengthened as a result. Dominance of the Mapam in turn would further antagonize American opinion, and this resentment might be vented on American Jews who would be charged with Communist sympathies.

...Regardless of disavowals by Jewish organizations, we must face the fact that Jews in this country are considered to have close ties with Israel. Public antipathy toward Israel would all too likely spill over into hostility toward American Jews. Anti-Semites and pro-Arabs in the USA would be quick to capitalize on such an opportunity.

A comprehensive public relations plan was proposed:

THE PROGRAM

In forestalling or counteracting unfavorable developments in public opinion, there are three main themes which should be stressed.

1. *Peace must be made and enforced by the UN*.
(a)...The UN and the great powers must be urged to use all means at their disposal to bring the warring parties to the peace table for the purpose of negotiating a settlement.
(b) Creation of a Middle-East defense system against communism depends on a prompt end to Israeli-Arab friction. Israel must be the anchor of this system.

2. *U.S. must support Israel as an outpost of democracy*.
(a) Jews are democracy's traditional allies. Recent example is the part played by Jews in World War II, in contrast to pro-Nazi perfidy on the part of Arabs.
(b) Unrest and misery in Middle-East serve the ends of communism. Arabs are traditionally and chronically in chaotic social condition, while Jews have created an oasis of industry, education and social welfare.
(c) *Israel's political and social structure constitutes the only democracy in the Middle East*.

3. *False and misleading Arab propaganda must be exposed*.
(a) Such problems as the internationalization of Jerusalem, Arab refugees and the Jordan Project, as well as border incidents, must be considered in the light of facts. These problems cannot be solved until the Arab propaganda which beclouds them is expelled.

> *In bringing these themes to the public, all the mass media should be brought into action; also the special media, particularly the religious press. This memorandum does not attempt to cover the details of these operations or to marshal the facts that must be gathered to support our informational campaign.*
>
> *To the utmost extent, non-Jewish and non-sectarian organizations should be used as spokesmen.*
>
> *The role of the Israeli embassy must be carefully considered; also that of the Zionist organizations, the rabbinical groups and the defense agencies.*
>
> *An important question to consider is the advisability of calling into conference a number of Zionist and other Jewish organizations to attempt to explore the possibility of cooperative action, at least in some areas, in a public relations program.*[278]

November 16, 1953 AJC executive director John Slawson met with Consul-General of Israel Avraham Harman for help in "developing a public opinion program to interpret Israel's problems to the American people, for the reason that opinions concerning Israel affect public attitudes toward American Jews."

Harman briefed Slawson on Israel's positions, telling him that the creation of Israel had been "A feat of colonization unique in history, which was accomplished without displacing anyone."[279]

A report in April 1954 on the progress of the program, which repeatedly contacted major and minor print and electronic media in the United States with information favorable to Israel, explained its rationale:

> *The major focus of this committee's activities during the five months of its existence, was the impact of the Middle East crisis on American public opinion. Most immediately we were concerned with the effect of any possible anti-Israel sentiment, stirred up by Kibya and*

---

[278] "Public Relations Factors in the Israel Situation," Oct 27, 1953, "Record of the American Jewish Committee in Re Palestine," Vol 4, AJC.

[279] Memo from Ethel C. Philips, "RE: Meeting with Mr. Avraham Harman, Consul-General of Israel, Monday, November 16, 3:00 P.M.," Nov. 17, 1953, "Israel, Foreign Affairs Department Collection, FAD. Reports on meeting with Israeli Consul General Avraham Harman, American news media on Israel, and American Jews and Israel, November-December 1953," ajcarchives.org. The report on "American news media on Israel" provides detailed "for" and "against" analysis of 162 editorials from the US newspapers about Israel's Qibya raid and the dispute over waters of the Jordan.

similar incidents in the news, on the position of American Jews, the assumption being that the general public associates American Jews with Israel.

It was decided,
> the (AJC) Public Information and Education Department would continue to carry on an educational program [promoting positive stories about Israel to American media] along the lines undertaken in recent months.[280]

The AJC was acting in reaction to consequences inadvertently foreseen by Moshe Shertok in March 1948, as he argued to UN Security Council members that so many "Jewish hostages throughout the world" would be a guarantee of the good behavior of the Jews of Palestine towards the Arabs after partition.[281]

Graphic in the AJC web site, June 2010, above news of the symbolic international flotilla to break the Gaza blockade. As time has passed, the organization has become more forthright about identifying with Israeli interpretations of events. (Original in color.)

---

280 Report by Sonya Kaufer, in "Alfred L. Bernheim to Staff Committee on Israel," April 21, 1954, "AJC Committees on Israel File, Foreign Affairs Department, FAD-1. Memoranda on relationship of American Jews to Israel, 1951-1955." ajcarchives.org.
281 "The United States Representative at the United Nations (Austin) to the Secretary," March 13, 1948, FRUS 1948, Volume V, Part II, page 716. "[Shertok said] It was obviously a basic principle in the self interest of the Jews to treat the Arabs fairly. There were too many Jewish hostages throughout the world. They would be living in a glass house in Palestine under the severe light of world public opinion."

Secret Peace Envoy to Egypt for Israel — 1954

BLAUSTEIN HAD a belief that in his role as a "third party" trusted by all sides, he could ease the state of war between Israel and Egypt and promote neighborly relations. In 1951, US State Department notes report,

> Mr. Blaustein said he wondered if there was anything he, as a non-Zionist American in no way associated with the Israel Government, could do to bring Egypt and Israel together. If he or someone like him could only talk with the Egyptians to ascertain their conditions for a peaceful settlement, it might be possible for him to persuade friends in Israel to make an offer along these lines. Mr. McGhee said that he would try to arrange a meeting between Mr. Blaustein and the Egyptian Ambassador. He did not know how productive the meeting would be but thought that it was worth trying.[282]

Jacob met with the ambassador in June, and reported to assistant Secretary of State George McGhee, "He had told the Egyptian Ambassador that he was a non-Zionist, but not an anti-Zionist. He was not a member of any Zionist organization nor a supporter of the more radical aspects of Zionism. He was eager for peace in the Near East area and hoped that the ECA [Marshall Plan] aid could be extended to the area in order to fight Communism."[283]

In 1954, assistant Secretary of State Henry A. Byroade arranged for JB to have secret talks with Egyptian Ambassador Ahmed Hussein in Washington in May and General Mahmud Riad when he was in New York City in October 1954.[284]

Blaustein reported that Hussein told Blaustein that "Byroade had given him JB's background - industrialist, helpful to Israel but a non-Zionist, fair and objective and top American citizen."

---

[282] "Memorandum of Conversation, by the Acting Officer in Charge of Lebanon-Syria-Iraq Affairs (Barrow) CONFIDENTIAL [WASHINGTON,] May 7, 1951," FRUS 1951, Vol. V, page 666.

[283] "Memorandum of Conversation, by the Assistant Secretary of State for Near Eastern, South Asian, and African Affairs (McGhee) CONFIDENTIAL [WASHINGTON,] June 11, 1951," page 708, *ibid*.

[284] "MEMO Conference JB with Ahmed Hussein, Egyptian Ambassador to the U.S. (Washington) May 12, 1954," and "MEMO JB (Washington) to Parker Hart (Washington), October 12, 1954," Box 1.73, folder 1460 "AJC Byroade, General Henry A. 1951-1970," JHU.

> ...Hussein agreed with JB that it would be better if the Arabs instead of making antagonism and lack of peace with Israel its main consideration, got that past them and concentrated on the main enemy, Russia. ...Hussein said he personally agreed with JB that aside from a limited number of radical elements in Israel, Israel is not needing or looking for expansion of territory.

One of the opinions the ambassador confided to Jacob was that if peace was going to develop, the Israelis were going to have to make some accommodation for the displaced Arab refugees.

> ...Hussein said he did not believe Israel could repatriate the Arab refugees - but that some of them had to be repatriated on former Palestine soil. ...From this statement and other comments, JB got the impression...that Hussein was implying that Israel should give up some of its territory for this purpose. ...Hussein said it was highly desirable to work for peace but he said there was only one way to approach it and that was through unofficial channels - with the knowledge and approval of the respective governments. Thus, he said, from what Byroade told him about JB, he assumes Israel would be willing for JB to serve unofficially for it.

When Blaustein reported on the meeting with Ambassador Hussein to Byroade, "Byroade said this was the best news he had had in a long time. He is delighted with it and would like to see the talks get under way promptly. ...JB said he has now checked with the Israeli government and they are very eager for JB to do so."[285]

At the same time, elements of the Israeli Defense Ministry were pursuing "Operation Susannah," using 11 Egyptian Jews to plant firebombs in Egypt in Post Offices, British and American buildings, and a movie theater, in a campaign intended to damage British confidence in the stability of the new post-King Farouk Egyptian nationalist government and convince the British to not remove their troops from the Suez Canal Zone.

While Israel's Foreign Ministry was using Blaustein and the Americans to start a relationship with Egypt's new government, a sub-cabinet part of

---

[285]"MEMO Conference Henry A. Byroade with JB (Washington, D.C.) May 24, 1954," ibid.

the Defense Ministry — or Minister Pinhas Lavon himself, depending on which story is true — was running this contrary plan.

In what became knows as the "Lavon Affair," the Egyptian Jews used as agents for Israel were arrested, publicly tried and convicted, and their employment by Israel exposed. This damaged the position of the Egyptian Jewish community.

Blaustein reached Paris in November 1954 on his way to meet Gamel Abdel Nasser, but received a message from the US embassy in Cairo, "The Foreign Office officially advised the Embassy this morning that it will not be possible for the Prime Minister to see him. GOE reports that it has no objection to his visit to Egypt as a tourist. Comment: The Embassy believes that the above answer can be accounted for by the current difficulties with the Muslim brotherhood which, although it is under heavy pressure, would be quick to use any contact between Nasir [sic] and Blaustein to the former's disadvantage."[286]

Political control in Egypt was in turmoil, with struggles between Nasser and Mohammed Naguib, and assertions from communist and Muslim Brotherhood forces.

The next year, Blaustein again tried to arrange a meeting with the Egyptian leader.
> *I have a definite feeling, (shared in the other quarters and in which I believe you also concur) that if I could have a heart to heart talk with Premier Nasser and then with the other parties, much progress could be made in clearing away the troublesome underbrush that stands in the way of better understanding between the neighbors. I feel quite sure that my objective approach, added to the confidence I enjoy, could be helpful all-around.*[287]

Byroade replied that the situation had deteriorated in the Cairo political scene, since JB's contacts with the Egyptians the previous year, because of the Israeli raid on Gaza of February 28, 1955.
> *I regret to say that situation has hardened here considerably from that which existed prior to the incident that occurred the day after my arrival here and with which you are familiar. I feel there is still some*

---

[286] "11/9/54 Record of message received in Paris from Ambassador in Cairo," *ibid.*
[287] Letter, JB to Henry A. Byroade, American Embassy, Cairo, July 16, 1955, *ibid.*

> objectivity remaining but more time will have to be put between us and that incident before much can be profitably done.[288]

The day after Byroade's arrival in Cairo as ambassador, the Israeli army had conducted a raid on an Egyptian military base in the Gaza strip, killing approximately 40 people. The United Nations Security Council unanimously condemned the attack on March 29 in Resolution 106. After the raid, US delegate James J. Wadsworth said that the raid was "indefensible from any standpoint" and that "We oppose any policy of reprisal and retaliation."[289]

---

[288] Letter, Henry A. Byroade, Ambassador, to Jacob Blaustein, August 5, 1955, *ibid.*
[289] "U.N. Asks Egypt and Israel To Avoid Further Violence," New York Times, March 5, 1955.

A White House Visit — 1950

A HALF-HOUR Blaustein visit with Pres. Truman in the White House, Sept. 28, 1950 was reported in detail in Blaustein's files, one of many recorded with Truman and with State Department officials.

The meeting begins with Truman regretting the recent congressional override of his veto of the (McCarran) Internal Security Act, and Blaustein commiserating. "Truman said what disturbs him is that this bill is probably unconstitutional, will be most difficult to enforce, and in a number of respects will aid Communism rather than hinder it."

Blaustein then said he had just come from a meeting of the National Petroleum Council (NPC)[*], and needed to ask Truman to issue an exemption so that oil industry executives recruited to join the council could receive "supplementary pay from their present connections" to not suffer financially by joining the NPC. "The President said that under the Defense Act he personally has a right to make exceptions to do what JB has in mind and that he will do so in some cases but that he is going to have all cases submitted to him personally. The President said that he knew a lot about this $1.00 a year man business as a result of his investigation when in the Senate of operations during the last war and the President said he did not intend to have people in government primarily for the purpose of fattening their own business operations.

"JB asked the President whether he then could tell the NPC people that the President was willing to make some specific exceptions where in his own opinion he felt they were justified, and the President said JB might do so."

The majority of the meeting concerned Israel. The memo records that Blaustein began by saying the AJC
> is a non-Zionist organization with an objective but sympathetic approach to Israel; and that JB has maintained a close contact with President Weizmann, Prime Minister Ben-Gurion and other Israeli officials, with our own State Department here and our American Embassy in Israel, and that the President further knew, of course, that all this has been within the framework of our American interests. Truman said that he understood that fully."

---

[*] Blaustein was a member of the NPC, and previously of the (WWII) Petroleum Industry War Council, both oil industry/government planning organs.

> "JB said that he mentioned in the last conference with the President that he is assured Israel can be counted on 100% as an ally of the United States, both politically and militarily.ᵗ
>
> "The President said he believed that to be so."

Blaustein told Truman that Israeli officials had received a report that "the near East in emergency would be left to the responsibility of the British against which the President had given JB an assurance that there was no such plan with the authorization to JB to so state to Israeli officials."‡

After discussing the "humanitarian aspects" of Israel's high rate of immigration from "Iron Curtain" countries, Blaustein at length described the "manpower" aspects of the immigration "which could be very important to our country as well as Israel under certain circumstances."

> JB said that frankly Ben-Gurion had told him that by this immigration process he wants to get more youth of military age so that in the event of world conflict they would be available to fight. Ben-Gurion has a definite feeling therefore that the United States instead of discouraging immigration into Israel should encourage it and that JB also feels that we should in the case of Israel, if there is world conflict, want to save American boys as far as possible just the same as Russia is aiming to do with respect to its satellites, just the same, indeed, as the United States is aiming to do by supplying arms and training our allies.
>
> The President said that JB was right about that and indeed that is what we are doing in our country to which JB added "and unfortunately, that appears to be what we may have to be doing in Germany". The president said we were not militarizing Germany yet but he, too, was aware that the time would come when we would have to do so.
>
> JB said that Ben-Gurion feels that the United States would be justified in helping financially to encourage

---

† See "BEN-GURION BACKED ON SHIFT TO WEST; Israeli Parliament, by 63 to 16, Votes for Policy," New York Times, Nov. 6, 1951, page 16.
‡ Blaustein later also relayed Truman's answer to Assistant Secretary of State McGhee.

immigration and militarily train these youths and that Ben-Gurion feels that no only will this save American youth in the event of conflict but that this program could actually be carried on by the United States at a lower cost to itself than to put in our own American troops. JB said Ben-Gurion had gotten some figure that it cost the United States something like $3,000. per man to train and maintain each member of a troop in a foreign country. JB did not mention that Ben-Gurion had told him that Israel, by adequate immigration, hopes to be able to get about 150,000 additional persons of military age.§

The President said that he could see the force of what JB was saying and that he would give that aspect earnest consideration.

JB said also that he believed the United States should permit more Israeli boys to train here....JB and Ben-Gurion were not saying less Arabs should be trained here but feel quite definitely that for our own United States interests in the Near East, more Israeli boys should be trained here.

The President said he would also give that consideration.

Blaustein began talking about Israel's need for loans and aid. *As a corollary to Israel being a bastion of democracy in the Near East and our ally, politically and militarily, it is essential for them to become a viable, self-supporting state....* [He said they would need] *outside financial aid*

---

§ David Ben Gurion brought the same message to Secretary of State Dean Acheson the next May. "Prime Minister said that Israel has the capacity to defend itself and to take part in the defense of the Middle East; Israel has the manpower and the industrial capacity; the manpower-is growing rapidly and is now twice what it had been on the establishment of the State. As a result of the steady inflow of immigrants there is now in Israel a larger proportion of people between the ages of fifteen and forty than in most countries; Israel has a small standing army but has taken measures to train large reserves." "Memorandum of Conversation, by the Secretary of State SECRET [WASHINGTON,] May 8, 1951," FRUS 1951, Vol. V, page 667. The theme of *aliyah* to build military strength continued. "Ben Gurion Calls Big Influx Vital," New York Times, Aug. 12, 1957, page 3. "To insure her security, Israel must take in at least 2,000,000 more immigrants during the next few years, Premier David Ben-Gurion said tonight"

> *for several more years to come.* [In addition to aid from world Jewry], *particularly in the United States...Additional government aid is required, and it would seem that the United States would be justified in supplying additional financial assistance to Israel, both through some form of ECA* [Marshall Plan] *and through Export-Import Bank loans....*
>
> *The President said here again he sees the parallel JB is drawing between other countries friendly to the United States and Israel and he would give that full and early consideration.*

Blaustein touched on the ambiguities inherent in American Jewish lobbying for the State of Israel, in a passage that illustrates that he was successful because he was a trusted participant in American economic life and planning.

> *JB said that he hoped from these last two conferences that the President would not get the impression that JB was trying to be only a special pleader for Israel but JB really feels that these matters in his letter and his discussions are of substantial concern to our own government as well as Israel....*
>
> *The President said that he knew JB was interested primarily in our own country and institutions other than Israel and in humanity in general and that he had a great admiration for JB because of that, and when the President realizes that JB additionally is a big industrialist with much else he could be doing, the President can't refrain from saying that he considers JB one of our great American citizens.*
>
> *The President said that with the splendid reputation JB has, not only in the humanitarian field, but in industry, he believes JB can be of immeasurable help to our government in getting industry what is right and proper and that he will be calling on JB for assistance in that direction especially the economic mobilization of prices and wages, etc., gets under way, and that* [Sen.] *Stuart Symington would be calling on JB for that aid.*

> *The President said he really has tried to refrain from putting on economic controls for two reasons: (1) because he does not want to have any more rigorous set-up than is absolutely necessary....and (2) because he does not want Russia to then be able to say to the rest of the world that the acts of the United States are proving that the United States is preparing to take the initiative in a war. The President said though that he would have to shortly apply economic control.*[290]

In a conference with Assistant Secretary of State George C. McGhee and his staff the following month, Blaustein continued lobbying for US aid to Israel to strengthen the "moderate" forces in Israel, the Mapai (the ruling Labor Zionist/Socialist Party). "JB urged upon them that it would be most helpful if the United States would do something promptly that would strengthen Weizmann's and Ben-Gurion's hands in the election. JB said just as the United States did with the $100,000,000 loan at the time of the first elections in Israel. They said they saw that."[291]

A Jan 10, 1949 Blaustein letter congratulates President Truman on his State of the Union speech and suggestions on tidelands oil, excess profits tax, labor act, and Israel. The letter says "early *de jure* recognition is essential —and I was encouraged by your statement that this will be done promptly after the Israeli elections this month."

The letter continues, "It was also encouraging to get your favorable comment to the suggestion that our government department diligently expedite the loan to Israel." In an example of US actions advocated to influence Israeli electorate in a favorable way, Blaustein requests that the loan and recognition be announced, as "[it] occurs to me it would be most helpful to peace and to the further strengthening of the hand of Dr. Weizmann and the present Provisional Government in Israel in the forthcoming elections.."[292]

---

[290]"MEMO JB Conference with President Truman September 28, 1950," Box 1.30, folder 416 "AJC - Truman, President," 12 pages, JHU.
[291]"MEMO JB Conference with McGhee, Berry & Rockwell (Washington), October 17, 1950," page 3, Box 1.56, folder 991 "McGhee Asst. Secretary of State 1949-1950," JHU.
[292]Jacob Blaustein to Harry S. Truman, January 10, 1949, Box 3.16, folder C-3-10 "VIP letters," JHU.

Restraining Nationalist Zionism: "Our Committee will be obliged to issue a severe, critical statement."

AFTER STATEHOOD, while the AJC was working to strengthen Israel's positions with the US government and counter Palestinian Arab claims of injury, it was struggling with the Ben Gurion's proclamations that Israel represented the Jewish people, and that Jews living abroad now should return. A 1942 conference with Ben Gurion to plan AJC coordination with the Jewish Agency and the 1946 decision of the AJC to support Partition had been, it understood, in exchange for the Zionist Organization agreeing to moderate its vision of a Jewish state to an American-style non-nationalist entity.

In a May 31, 1949 letter Proskauer (former AJC President) to Blaustein (current President) wrote,

> I am much bothered by the speech which Elath made at ZOA [Zionist Organization of America] as it was printed in yesterday's newspapers. [Added in pencil: "NY Times article attached."[293]] He came out with a strong plea for Americans to go to Israel as pioneers. I shall try to reach him on the telephone today and ferret out what in hell prompted him to do such a stupid thing. He is just playing into [Lessing] Rosenwald's hands and hurting us all very much. I am going to try to work out some kind of quasi retraction from him....
> Would you rather take this job over yourself, or do you perhaps
> disapprove of what I am doing? I think the decision must be yours.
> Please telegraph me in answer to this.[294]

---

[293] "CONTINUING NEED FOR ZIONISM SEEN; Elath, Silver Call for Strong Movement to Foster Jewish Culture in All Lands," New York Times, May 30, 1949, Page 6. (The article also reports Zionist Organization vice president Herman L. Weisman "emphasized that Zionism should be a factor in the building of Israel so that it would 'fulfill its historic mission of being a standard bearer of Western civilization in the Middle East.'" In 1950, the *Times* reported, "Dr. James G. Heller, rabbi of Issac M. Wise Temple of Cincinnati, asserted that although Jews were entering Israel from the East in large numbers, 'the spirit of the land must be of the West.'" "Mrs. Myerson in Plea for U.S. Funds, Labor," May 30, 1950, page 21.)

[294] Joseph Proskauer to Jacob Blaustein, letter. May 31, 1949, Box 2.1 folder A-1-18 "AJC Emigration to Israel 1949," JHU.

The *New York Times* article reported Israeli ambassador to the United States Elath telling the ZOA annual meeting,
> The people of Israel and Jews throughout the world, he [Elath] said, need a Zionist movement that continues to foster Jewish culture, pointing out that only by this method can Israel expect to receive immigrants who will continue the traditions of the Zionist pioneers.
>
> Turning to the economic conditions in his country, Mr. Elath said: "Israel needs not only American money, American know-how, but also pioneers from this country who should come to settle in Israel and join us in the building of our new state."

June 2, Blaustein telegraphed to Proskauer,
> RELET. PLEASE DO PHONE ELATH. WILL BE MOST HELPFUL. I PLANNING ANOTHER TALK WITH HIM REGARDING VARIOUS MATTER AS FOLLOW-UP ISRAEL TRIP AND WILL ALSO MENTION THIS ITEM ON WHICH BEN GURION HAD GIVEN ME SOME ASSURANCES.[295]

In a June 3, 1949 letter Blaustein describes calling Ambassador Elath.
> I told him that one of the things that disturbed us when we were in Israel was the notion held by quite a number there that American Jews are insecure here and will ultimately have to flee to Israel -- which of course is utter nonsense.
> I also told him that we had fully discussed this situation with Ben-Gurion at Tiberias and had pointed out to him that any campaign over here to get American youth to go to Israel as pioneers -- especially if a fear complex were injected, and even without it --would be resented by American Jews (Zionists as well as others) and would lose Israel much financial and other support.
> Elath did, however, agree to send me promptly a clarifying letter, --
> which he did and copy is enclosed.
> This letter I think will be helpful, but it does not alter the fact that this situation, as well as a few others, will require careful vigilance on our part.[296]

---

[295] Jacob Blaustein to Joseph Proskauer, telegram, June 2, 1949, *ibid*.
[296] Blaustein to Proskauer, letter, June 3, 1949, *ibid*.

The issue of encouragement of American *aliyah* (emigration) to Israel simmered. October 14, 1949, Blaustein telegraphed Foreign Min. Moshe Sharett in Tel Aviv:

> I HAVE JUST CABLED PRIME MINISTER BEN GURION AS FOLLOW QUOTE I AM DISTRESSED NOT TO HAVE RECEIVED REPLY TO MY SEPTEMBER 19TH LETTER* REGARDING YOUR REPORTED STATEMENT PROPAGANDIZING FOR EMIGRATION OF AMERICAN JEWS TO ISRAEL. SINCE THEN THERE HAS BEEN EVEN INCREASED CONSTERNATION HERE, AMONG BOTH ZIONISTS AND NON-ZIONISTS, DUE TO IT AND THE FUTILITY AND DANGER OF THE THEORY IMPLICIT IN IT. MANY OF OUR OWN MEMBERS ARE INSISTING THAT UNLESS YOU DISCLAIM ANY INTENTION ON THE PART OF THE STATE OF ISRAEL TO INTERFERE WITH THE LIFE OF AMERICAN JEWRY, THE AMERICAN JEWISH COMMITTEE AT ITS FORTHCOMING MEETING NEXT WEEK MUST TAKE APPROPRIATE ACTION TO UNDO THE HARM OT THE POSITION OF AMERICAN JEWRY RESULTING FROM YOUR REPORTED STATEMENT...I NEED AND ANXIOUSLY AWAIT YOUR REPLY BY OCT. 19TH....JACOB BLAUSTEIN, PRESIDENT, AMERICAN JEWISH COMMITTEE"[297]

In a seven-page phone transcript Oct. 18, 1949 of a conversation with Elath, Blaustein wants a better public correction of remarks about American Jewish "pioneers" to Israel. In a four-page phone transcript October 20, Blaustein says, "I mean, I'm telling you from a public relations standpoint, you don't seem to be able to get the point I'm making." He mentions that Lessing Rosenwald followers on AJC Executive Committee "are coming there with blood in their eyes."[298]

In an October 1949 letter from Blaustein to Proskauer, he writes that in publicly objecting to Ben Gurion's reported call for American Jewish youth to "return" to Israel, "We would be saying we were misled (-not that I disagree with telling that if we finally fail in correcting the situation)."

In the letter, Blaustein clearly describes the demands of public Jewish unity that constrained denunciation of Zionist identification of the State

---
* See page 185.
[297] Blaustein to Eliahu Elath, telegram, Oct. 18, 1949, *ibid*.
[298] Box 2.1, Folder A-1-11 "AJC BEN GURION 1949-1964," JHU.

of Israel with the religious promise of *kibbutz galuyyot* — "Gathering of the Exiles."

Jacob lists the following consequences that argued against public announcement that the AJC had been misled:

- *We will in effect be changing our position as far as wholeheartedly backing the State of Israel is concerned; and will be contributing - even though certain Israeli and Zionist leaders will be the primary cause - toward a breakdown of the unity in the community which we in such large measure helped bring about.*
- *We will be adversely affecting contributions to the United Jewish Appeal and possible investments in Israel - which means that we will be jeopardizing the chances for Israel to be a viable, self-supporting State.*
- *We will be playing right into the hands of the American Council for Judaism, and furthering its program which as handled in the general press is conducive to anti-Semitism.*
- *We will be headed for renewed problems with our B'nai Brith - ADL partners and in the Joint Defense Appeal.*
- *We will undoubtedly be cutting our bridges with the Israeli officials and be losing such influence as we may now have, getting ourselves in that respect in the ineffective position of the American Council for Judaism.*

The letter concludes, "It therefore behooves us to be statesmanlike and to avoid to the extent we can the taking of any premature or false steps," and proposes concentrating "on obtaining if possible a clear-cut disavowal from Ben-Gurion, and I have indicated to Elath what might be done."

> *We have an obligation to our members and American Jewry that extends beyond the mere issuance of a statement....*
> *We are partly responsible for the State of Israel having come into being; and as I see it, we have an obligation to do everything we can to rectify any wrong acts or statements of Israel and its officials which might have an adverse impact on the American scene. We have been placed in a unique position that carries with it responsibility to maintain (if Israel's conduct will permit it) that relationship which will enable us to exert an influence for what is right and proper. We must not cast that opportunity aside...*

Blaustein tells Proskauer that he has talked with Ambassador Elath, and that Elath
> said he proposed to urge in the strongest terms that Sharett induce Ben-Gurion to let me have a prompt and satisfactory reply, stating that in the absence of same he fears our Committee will be obliged to issue a severe, critical statement.
>
> Elath and Eban are very much perturbed about this whole situation, and you will agree that it is helpful to have them fighting on the inside for our views in this matter based on their own convictions.[299]

An October 26 1949 memo from AJC's Simon Segal quoted a letter of Morris D. Waldman (AJC executive secretary, 1928-45):
> During our negotiations with the Zionist leaders -- at the time of the Weizmann-Stroock conferences -- at lunch alone with ben Gurion he said to me unequivocally that he realized that Jewish life must naturally evolve in every country in harmony with the particular conditions of each country, that he did not expect Jews outside of Palestine to be politically identified with that country, that he wanted Palestine to be the country only of those Jews who, like himself, live there. The statement he was recently reported to have made definitely contradicts the spirit and letter of the assurances he gave me in 1942.[300]

Jacob wrote in anger and exasperation to his wife Hilda, about a Nahum Goldmann statement at the 1953 World Jewish Congress which reportedly mentioned a "duty" of Jews to go to Israel, "it goes to show how alert we have to be with these people all the time."[301]

In 1960, the AJC protested a World Jewish Congress speech of Ben Gurion, where he quoted, "Whoever dwells outside the land of Israel is considered to have no God, the sages said," and of Western Jews warned that "Judaism faces death by a kiss — a slow and imperceptible decline into the abyss of assimilation."

---

[299] Jacob Blaustein to Joseph Proskauer, letter, Oct. 12, 1949, page 1-3, Box 2.21, folder C-2-23 "Proskauer, Judge Joseph M.," JHU.
[300] Simon Segal to Jacob Blaustein, memo, Oct. 26, 1949, Box 2.21, Folder A-1-11 "AJC BEN GURION 1949-1964," JHU
[301] Jacob Blaustein to Hilda Blaustein, August 7, 1953, File AA-1-56, JHU.

The AJC responded with their non-nationalist American conception of Jewish life:
> *Reaffirming the Committee's view that "emigration to Israel must be an act of free choice," the AJC stated that Mr. Ben-Gurion was committing a "grievous error" in attempting to interpret the obligations of Jewish religious belief and practice to Jews throughout the world. Judaism, the AJC declared, "is in fact a flourishing religion which, in democratic countries such as the United States, enjoys equal rights and opportunities with all other religions."*[302]

With varying success, the AJC pressed its concerns on other issues: Orthodox religious authority over personal matters such as marriage in Israel, the rights of Arabs and Jews from Arab countries in Israel, the continuing plight of Arab refugees, and Israel's Nationality Law, the Jewish "Right of Return."
> *The AJC has long regarded as undemocratic the preferred legal status given to Jews under the Nationality Law, which provides that a Jewish immigrant automatically acquires Israel citizenship on arrival in Israel, unless he signs a formal declaration refusing it.*[303]

As late as 1976, Jacob's son-in-law David Hirschhorn wrote, during the controversy over Jews leaving the Soviet Union with Israeli visas — the only available way they could leave the USSR — "dropping out" in Vienna and choosing other destinations, against the wishes of the Israeli government:
> *I would be distressed to find that decisions regarding the emigration of Soviet Jewry would be based on whether such Jews are prepared to immigrate to Israel only. As desirable as it is that Soviet Jews should immigrate to Israel, I have never understood that is our only objective. I have always worked on the premise that the program was based on our concern for the status of Jews in the Soviet Union and what might be done to assure their survival as Jews.*[304]

---
302 *In Vigilant Brotherhood*, AJC, 1964, pages 57-58.
303 *Ibid*, pages 49-51.
304 David Hirschhorn to Bert Gold, executive vice president, AJC, Aug. 20, 1976, in reaction to Aug. 18 article in the Baltimore Sun, "Israel considers refusing visas to Soviet Jews going to West". "Bertram Gold Boxes 1970s, Soviet Union - Spain," Box 196, AJC. My thanks to Fred Lazin of Ben Gurion University for pointing out this document to me.

The Ben Gurion-Blaustein "Exchange of Views" — 1950

Paula Ben Gurion, PM David Ben Gurion, Jacob Blaustein (speaking), Labor Minister Golda Myerson, Foreign Minister Moshe Sharett, August 23, 1950, at the King David Hotel, Jerusalem. (Photo: JHU)

By the distance of 60 years, it is difficult to clearly recognize the issue resolved by the Ben Gurion-Blaustein Exchange. It was provoked by ongoing announcements from leaders of the new State of Israel that *aliyah* (ascension, in Hebrew) to the Land of Israel (HaEretz) was expected from the Jews of the "west." Worse, possibly, was the implication of the statements that Jews owed Israel a sort of national loyalty.

As can be seen in the previous chapter, there was alarm and anger at Israeli statements. Although sympathetic to Jewish refugees finding safety and dignity in Palestine, the AJC was oriented to the struggle to make American society welcoming to full participation by Jews and other minorities, with a strong orientation to social justice. This goal had cognitive dissonance with rebuilding an ethnic Jewish enclave that would "negate the diaspora," as Zionist ideology asserted.

Oratory of Ben Gurion that had most provoked AJC anger was reported by the Jewish Telegraphic Agency news bulletin of September 1, 1949:

> *Our next task consists of bringing all Jews to Israel...*
> *We appeal chiefly to the youth in the United States and in other countries to help us achieve this big mission. We appeal to the parents to help us bring their children here. Even if they decline to help, we will bring the youth to Israel, but I hope that this will not be necessary.*

Blaustein reproached Ben Gurion that in Blaustein's visit earlier in the year, Ben Gurion had promised that "you did not expect and you would not indulge in any organized campaign for the immigration of American Jewish youth." Blaustein promised to "do what is in our power to call the attention of our fellow Jews of the United States to the futility and danger of the theory implicit in the speech attributed to you."[305]

Early in 1950, Jacob Blaustein castigated the idea, of some American Jews, of Israel as a refuge for American Jews:

> *...These frightened men do not learn from history that given emancipation, acceptance, and security, Jews and all other groups throughout modern history have readily sought to become an integral part of the countries of their birth or adoption. They forget that it is only anti-Semitism and political and social threats to their security that breeds separatism and nationalism among Jews.*
>
> *Our appointed task, therefore, is to work for the continued betterment, the broadening and deepening of American democracy, by the removal of discrimination, by the expansion of civil rights for all Americans, and by the continued improvement and enrichment of Jewish individuality and of Jewish communal life.*[306]

The view of the Jew as doomed to both fruitless assimilation and hostility, as Theodor Herzl had it, was an irrelevancy to the robust Jewish community of the United States.

In the ceremonial "Exchange of Views" of Prime Minister David Ben

---

[305] JB to Ben Gurion, September 19, 1949, in file "Israel/American Jews & Israel File, Foreign Affairs Department Collection, FAD-1, Memoranda and committee minutes on relationship of American Jews to Israel, 1948-1950," ajcarchives.org.

[306] Jacob Blaustein, *The Voice of Reason: Address by Jacob Blaustein, President, The American Jewish Committee, at the meeting of its Executive Committee, April 29, 1950*, booklet, 18 pages, The American Jewish Committee, pages 12-13.

Gurion and American Jewish Committee President Jacob Blaustein, Ben Gurion acknowledged and repeated what may seem self-evident facts:
1. that the State of Israel spoke only for its own citizens
2. that Jews in other countries had no political obligations to the State of Israel.

Further, Ben Gurion gave public recognition that the future of Israel depended on not damaging the health and security of the American Jews.
> It is most unfortunate that since our State came into being some confusion and misunderstanding should have arisen as regards the relationship between Israel and the Jewish communities abroad, in particular that of the United States. These misunderstandings are likely to alienate sympathies and create disharmony where friendship and close understanding are of vital necessity. To my mind, the position is perfectly clear. The Jews of the United States, as a community and as individuals, have only one political attachment and that is to the United States of America. ... Our success or failure depends in a large measure on our cooperation with, and on the strength of, the great Jewish community of the United States, and, we, therefore, are anxious that nothing should be said or done which could in the slightest degree undermine the sense of security and stability of American Jewry.

This passage was believed at the time to represent a Ben Gurion retreat from Israeli statements that American Jews, or at least their children, were expected to emigrate to Israel:
> In this connection let me say a word about immigration. We should like to see American Jews come and take part in our effort. We need their technical knowledge, their unrivaled experience, their spirit of enterprise, their bold vision, their "know-how." We need engineers, chemists, builders, work managers and technicians. The tasks which face us in this country are eminently such as would appeal to the American genius for technical development and social progress. But the decision as to whether they wish to come--permanently or temporarily--rests with the free discretion of each American Jew himself. It is entirely a matter of his own volition.... I believe I know something of the spirit of American Jewry among whom I lived for some years. I

am convinced that it will continue to make a major contribution towards our great effort of reconstruction, and I hope that the talks we have had with you during these last few days will make for even closer cooperation between our two communities.

Blaustein's part in the "Exchange" laid out the dynamic tension of American Jews supporting a state of Jews, but resisting the more grand conceptions of Israel as the "Jewish state":

The American Jewish community sees its fortunes tied to the fate of liberal democracy in the United States, sustained by its heritage, as Americans and as Jews.

...The American Jewish Committee has been active, as have other Jewish organizations in the United States, in rendering, within the framework of their American citizenship, every possible support to Israel...

...But we must, in a true spirit of friendliness, sound a note of caution to Israel and its leaders. Now that the birth pains are over, and even though Israel is undergoing growing pains, it must recognize that the matter of good-will between its citizens and those of other countries is a two-way street: that Israel also has a responsibility in this situation--a responsibility in terms of not affecting adversely the sensibilities of Jews who are citizens of other states by what it says or does. In this connection, you are realists and want facts and I would be less than frank if I did not point out to you that American Jews vigorously repudiate any suggestion or implication that they are in exile. American Jews--young and old alike, Zionists and non-Zionists alike--are profoundly attached to America. America welcomed their immigrant parents in their need. Under America's free institutions, they and their children have achieved that freedom and sense of security unknown for long centuries of travail. American Jews have truly become Americans; just as have all other oppressed groups that have ever come to America's shores. To American Jews, America is home.

...They believe in the future of a democratic society in the United States under which all citizens, irrespective of creed or race, can live on terms of equality.

...Harm has been done to the morale and to some extent to the sense of security of the American Jewish

> *community through unwise and unwarranted statements and appeals which ignore the feelings and aspirations of American Jewry.* [307]

In April 1961 in Israel, Blaustein and Ben Gurion issued a reaffirmation of the 1950 agreement.
> *It was agreed that everything should be done on both sides in order to obviate such misunderstandings in the future, so that it would be entirely clear to everybody concerned that the 1950 Agreement had lost none of its force and validity as far as either side is concerned. In particular Mr. Ben-Gurion undertook to do everything within his power to see to it that the Agreement is in future kept in spirit and in letter...*[308]

Reaffirmations of the agreement were obtained from succeeding Prime Ministers Levi Eshkol and Golda Meir.

The activities of the *Nefesh b'Nefesh* organization — supported by the quasi-governmental Jewish Agency — to promote immigration from United States, seem inconsistent with the agreement reached between Blaustein and the Israeli government. Unless the organization is effective, this may not become an issue for American Jews.

In 1974, a writer about the agreement commented, "Events, and life, have — at least for the time being — rendered the 1950 'Exchange' without substance."[309]

Assuming intrusive Israeli state actions affecting the United States and American Jews — similar to "Operation Susannah," the Jonathan Pollard affair, the AIPAC spying case; or especially obvious manipulations of the US political system — do not come to light and inflame the issue of Israeli claims to embody Jewish nationhood[310], the Ben Gurion-Blaustein Exchange may remain a dead letter.

---

307 For the full text of the "Exchange," see the American Jewish Year Book (1952), Vol. 53, pages 564-568, American Jewish Committee, New York-Jewish Publication Society, Philadelphia.
308 In Vigilant Brotherhood, AJC, 1964, page 70.
309 Charles S. Liebman, "Diaspora Influence on Israel: The Ben Gurion-Blaustein 'Exchange' and Its Aftermath," Jewish Social Studies, Vol. 36, No. 3/4, July-Oct.1974, page 280.
310 Sallai Meridor, Israeli ambassador to the United States, in a speech to the Anti-Defamation League (ADL), in Washington, D.C., stated with satisfaction that Israel was a successful state "with a strong army to protect every Jew on the planet." April 14, 2008, at 32:30, rtsp://video1.c-span.org/project/intl/intlo41408_meridor.rm

Jacob Blaustein representing the US at the United Nations General Assembly in 1955. (Photo: JHU)

Identification with Zionism as Jewish Identity

In 1962 Joseph Proskauer explained that the American Jewish Committee's difference from Zionist doctrine was by design not publicly exposed and debated after statehood. The AJC choose to not clash with Jews who were committed to Israel statehood as a "Jewish" article of faith:

> We do not always agree with the Israelis and occasionally we get overheated statements about the Jews in the Diaspora, "The Jews must return to Israel." There are two ways of meeting that. One is to denounce all Zionists in the public press and feed the anti-Semites with ammunition that a group of Jews is charging fellow Jews with a lack of patriotism. The other is to send Jacob Blaustein to Jerusalem and have him, with his great tact and diplomacy, secure from Mr. Ben-Gurion a satisfactory statement consonant with our fundamental position that we can have no political affiliation with the State of Israel.[311]

In the same speech, Proskauer propounded at length his doctrine of a particular character of American Judaism that had escaped some "old-world" bounds:

> Some years ago -- and I had just become your President -- we had to meet the challenge of an organization that wished to create a national Sanhedrin that, by majority vote, would arrogate to itself power to speak for every Jew in America. Risking our very existence we fought this tyranny over ideas.[312] Recognition of the correctness of our views led to the destruction of that organization. That was right conduct. I am confident that every organization in the future that endeavors to create for itself the right to dominate the ideas of a minority will be rejected by the Jews of America once the way is made

---

311 "Six Decades of Public Service: Judge Joseph M. Proskauer Sums Up," American Jewish Committee, 1963, 8-page booklet, file C- 2-23 "Proskauer, Judge Joseph M.," JHU.

312 Proskauer may be referring to what became for a short number of years the American Jewish Conference. "On principle, the American Jewish Committee is unalterably opposed to any plan that would seem to set up the Jews as a separate political enclave, and your project, with its local and regional delegates, its elaborate electoral machinery, and its very title 'American Jewish Assembly' will certainly have this implication." Letter from Joseph Proskauer to Henry Monsky, March 16, 1943, quoted in Nathan Schachner, *The Price of Liberty*, AJC(publisher), 1948, page 145.

clear to them. The spirit of internal Jewish bigotry which expelled Spinoza from the brotherhood of Israel and brought Uriel Acosta prostrate to his death, was rooted out in the Jewish life of this free America.

The American Jewish Committee focused on Jewish learning and identity in the context of living as Americans. American Jews "cannot orient their life to activities halfway around the world," wrote philosopher Sidney Hook in an article in the 1946 AJC Annual Report.[313]

In a 1940 essay, psychologist Kurt Lewin may have hinted at the "royal road" out of uncertainty that Zionism may serve for Jews, and explained the tenacious grip of otherwise indifferent Jews to the concept of having "a country."

Not the <u>belonging to many groups</u> is the cause of the difficulty, but an <u>uncertainty</u> of belongingness.... For the modern Jew there exists an additional factor to increase his uncertainty. He is frequently uncertain about the way he belongs to the Jewish group, and to what degree. Especially since religion has become a less important social matter, it is rather difficult to describe positively the character of the Jewish group as a whole. A religious group with many atheists? A Jewish race with a great diversity of racial qualities among its members? A nation without a state or a territory of its own containing the majority of its people? A group combined by one culture and tradition but actually having in most respects the different values and ideals of the nations in which it lives? There are, I think, few chores more bewildering than that of determining positively the character of the Jewish group.... No wonder many Jews are uncertain about what it means to belong to the Jewish group...[314]

According to a 1990 AJC publication attempting to quantify American Jewish characteristics,

...it does seem that some attitudes, beliefs, and practices emerge as common denominators of American Jewish identity, particularly those that aim for the continuation of the Jewish people through <u>ties of kinship</u>, <u>religion</u>, and

---

313 "Values in Jewish Living" by Sidney Hook, Philosophy Department, Washington Square College, NYU, 40th Annual Report of the AJC(1946), pages 45-49, Box 1.24, folder 332 "American Jewish Committee Executive Committee Reports 1943-1955," JHU.

314 Kurt Lewin, Resolving Social Conflicts, Harper & Row, New York, 1948, page 179-180.

> *a common commitment to the welfare of Jewish people everywhere <u>and to the State of Israel</u>.*³¹⁵

The former Zionist Rabbi Morris S. Lazaron, of Baltimore, had a dour view of this process of the Zionization of Judaism:

> *Zionism insinuated itself into American Jewish life in the guise of philanthropy, and now in these later years it is even more its nationalist philosophy expressed in this country under the guise of promoting 'Jewishness,' 'Jewish unity,' 'Jewish education,' and 'Democracy in community life.' ...Finally I came to the conclusion that the Zionists were using Jewish need only to exploit their political goals. Every sacred feeling of the Jew, every instinct of humanity, every deep-rooted anxiety for family, every cherished memory became an instrument to be used for the promotion of the Zionist cause.*³¹⁶

Former AJC executive secretary Morris D. Waldman wrote in 1953, "A program of education [of American Jews] will be necessary to convince them that political Zionism based on the theory that the Jewish people are a 'homeless people' living in 'exile' is false and dangerous doctrine, threatening the position of Jews everywhere including the U.S...."³¹⁷

Bitterness and mistrust of rabbis such as Lazaron, toward Zionist intentions, was not unusual. In 1917, Seattle Rabbi Samuel Koch of Temple de Hirsch wrote angrily, after being asked repeatedly, on short notice, to accommodate Zionist speakers at the synagogue — in this case, "Professor Felix Frankfurter of Harvard": "The <u>indirection</u> of the telegram is characteristic of Zionist practice in general."³¹⁸

---

315 Perry London and Barry Chazan, "Psychology and Jewish Identity Education," American Jewish Committee Institute of Human Relations, 1990, page 13. Emphasis added.
316 Rabbi Morris S. Lazaron, "Why I Was a Zionist and Why I Now am Not," excerpt from his unpublished autobiography, *Generations* magazine (2007/2008), the journal of the Jewish Museum of Maryland, Baltimore, pages 45, 48.
317 Waldman, *Nor By Power*, page 271.
318 Samuel Koch to Henry Pickard, November 23, 1917, Temple de Hirsch Sinai records, Accession No. 2370-018, box 1, file 17, University of Washington Library, Special Collections.

"Well, it is probably the Indians." — May 1949

Beginning in 1946, when the AJC reluctantly joined with the Jewish Agency to lobby for Partition, it maintained close consultation with the US government, including with Blaustein's friend President Truman, on issues important to the Zionists, and later, the State of Israel. This passage from a phone conversation between Blaustein and Simon Segal of the AJC reflects the questions he was hearing from the Truman administration about the Israeli refusal to allow return of Arab war refugees:

> *JB[Jacob Blaustein]: Simon, let me ask you something. One of the big things that is disturbing the White House is the attitude toward the Arab refugees and there is still a good deal to do to try to serve in that connection. Now then, some people have told me that what Israel has been doing with respect to the Arab refugees, has precedence in what our country has done in certain situations but I don't know just what situations. Do you? Do you know at anytime when our country had anything similar to this and acted similarly?*
>
> *S[Simon Segal]: Acted similarly?*
>
> *JB: Yes.*
>
> *S: Oh, I don't know. (Indistinct). Maybe they are referring to the Indians.*
>
> *JB: I don't know what they're talking about but I have had several people say to me but they don't give me the particulars.*
>
> *S: Well, it is probably the Indians.*
>
> *JB: Well, the Indians.*
>
> *S: (Indistinct) ... we have been expelling them.*
>
> *JB: Well, that we haven't been making our shores, I guess, available. I don't know. Once they've left I should think that's the principle involved. That once people leave here, we don't necessarily welcome them back. Now, have there been any incidents like that?*
>
> *S: None as I know of. Maybe they are referring to the British who have left during the Revolutionary War, you*

know. They went to Canada. I don't know of any who wanted to come back and we didn't let them come back.

JB: Look here, Simon. Think about it a little bit this afternoon and if anything --- because that would be a darn good point to make if I could give a really good example. Think about that a bit. Now one more thing. Did you ever get a reaction from the Israeli people about the McG[h]ee Report; the thing that Ethridge wants us to try to push through?

S: Well, they're against it. Yes.

JB: They're against it?

S: Well, they are not in favor of any Marshall Plan.

JB: The Marshall Plan, of course, would place them in a position of...

S: (Indistinct)

JB: But does McG[h]ee, in his report, make clearly the point that it is impossible to expect the Israelis to bring all those Arab refugees back. Ethridge told me that it did.

S: Well, I asked Joel Wolfson to check that report. He may be able to tell you. If he has it, he will give it to you tomorrow morning. Are you going to see him tomorrow?

JB: I will see him but it will be after the meeting with the President.

S: After the meeting?

JB: Yeah.

S: Well, maybe before the meeting, -- if he can get it before the meeting, he will bring it to you.

JB: No. No. I'll tell you. If he can get it before the meeting, he better phone me today and let me know. In other words, ask him to try to get a copy.[319]

---

[319] MEMO PHONE CONVERSATION JB TO SIMON SEGAL, AJC director of foreign affairs, May 17, 1949, Box 1.30 folder 416 "AJC - Truman, President," JHU. First half of phone call is discussion of probable appointment of John J. McCloy as US High Commissioner for Germany, and of Ralph Bunche, successor to assassinated UN

Donald Neff in his book *Fallen Pillars* tells the story of the above-referenced efforts of US coordinator on Palestine refugees (and assistant secretary of state) George McGhee and American member of the UN Palestine Conciliation Commission Mark Ethridge to effect Israeli repatriation of at least some Arab refugees.[320]

Neff notes McGhee's account of his August defeat on the issue, after presenting a State Department ultimatum that some Export-Import Bank funds to Israel would be delayed unless some Arab refugees could return:

I asked the ambassador [Eliahu Elath] to lunch with me at the Metropolitan Club and put our decision to him in the most tactful and objective way I could....The ambassador looked me straight in the eye and said, in essence, that I wouldn't get by with this move, that he would stop it....Within an hour of my return to my office I received a message from the White House that the President wished to dissociate himself from any withholding of the Ex-Im Bank loan.[321]

Neff cites a July cable from the American consul in Jerusalem:

Israel eventually intends to obtain all of Palestine...will accomplish this objective gradually and without the use of force in the immediate future.

Israel is convinced of its ability to "induce" the United States to abandon its present insistence on repatriation of refugees and territorial changes. From experience in the past, officials state confidently "you will change your mind," and the press cites instances of the effectiveness of organized Jewish propaganda in the US.[322]

The cable also makes the point that the Israelis were in no position by that point to offer any right of return to refugees:

The State of Israel has no intention of allowing the return of any appreciable number of refugees except, perhaps, in return for additional territory. By this date there is much truth in the Israel contention that their return is

---

Palestine mediator Bernadotte.
320 Donald Neff, *Fallen Pillars: US Policy towards Palestine and Israel Since 1945*, Institute for Palestine Studies, Washington, DC, 1995, page 74-77.
321 George McGhee, *Envoy to the Middle World: Adventures in Diplomacy*, Harper & Row, New York, 1983, page 37.
322 "The Consul at Jerusalem (Burdett) to the Secretary of State, Secret, Jerusalem, July 6, 1949," FRUS 1949, Volume VI, page 1204

> *physically impossible. Arab houses and villages, including those in areas not given Israel by the partition decision, have been occupied to a large extent by new immigrants. Others have been deliberately destroyed. There is practically no room left. Arab quarters in Jerusalem, until recently a military zone, are now almost full and new immigrants are pouring in steadily.*[323]

In February 1949, US ambassador McDonald observed the Arab refugees' property was already taken:
> *Though the Israeli spokesmen do not say so, the unprecedentedly rapid influx of Jewish refugees during 1948 and the plan to admit a quarter of a million more in 1949 will, if carried out, fill all or almost all of the houses and business properties previously held by Arab refugees. Arab unoccupied farms will similarly, though not to quite the same degree, be occupied by the recent or expected Jewish refugees. Hence, there will be almost no residence or business property and only a limited number of farms to which Arab refugees can hope to return.*[324]

In October 1949, *Jewish Newsletter* editor William Zukerman wrote:
> *It is not generally realized that as a result of the war Israel has occupied considerable land which belonged to the Arabs. The former inhabitants of the land have fled, and Jewish settlers have taken over their villages, homes, gardens, orchards and fields. It is the first time in the last two thousand years of Jewish history that Jews have been placed in such a position. How do they comport themselves as victors and conquerors?...*
> *According to Mr. Pinsky*, the Israelis as conquerors do not generally differ much from other conquerors. Most of the Jewish refugees who now occupy former Arab homes and villages do so "with the laughter of victors."...*
> *But--in this respect the story is unique--not all Israelis feel that way....Mr. Pinksy describes a visit he made to the village of Yazir, not from from Jaffa, which was taken over by the Israeli army and renamed*

---
[323] Page 1204, *ibid.*
[324] "The Special Representative of the United States in Israel (McDonald) to the Secretary of State, Secret, Tel Aviv, February 22, 1949," FRUS1949, Volume VI, page 762.
* Yiddish-American playwright David Pinski.

> *Hamishmar Sheva. The entire Arab population had left the village and none had been permitted to return.*
>
> *The houses, the furniture, the gardens and orchards have been retained in good condition and are now occupied by Jewish settlers, living in comparative opulence after years of camp life. Yet somehow they don't feel right....The "trouble" seems to be that most of these people are not native Israelis of the younger generation, but former refugees from Poland, Czechoslovakia and other parts of Europe who were themselves refugees....they feel that they are enjoying something which is not theirs and their peace of mind is gone.*[325]

Harry Greenstein of Baltimore, an adviser on Jewish affairs to the US Occupation Forces in Germany and Austria, made two visits to Israel and observed the use of Arab properties. After an April 1949 visit to Israel, Greenstein reported,

> *Prior to the creation of the Jewish State, sixty-thousand Arabs lived in Jaffa. As a result of recent hostilities practically all of them evacuated the city. Approximately forty-thousand Jews occupy their homes.*
>
> *It is impossible to absorb any more Jews in Jaffa. Every inch of space is already occupied. While true that sixty-thousand Arabs formerly lived in Jaffa, it must be remembered that many of the buildings were destroyed which reduced available housing.*[326]

In October he noted in a booklet, a copy of which was given with a personal inscription to Blaustein:

> *Sixty-three new settlements have been started since the creation of the state. Thirty-seven of these were set up in former Arab villages.*[327]

In April 1949, Greenstein met in Tel Aviv with Blaustein, who along with Irving Engel, Dr. Simon Segal, and Zach Shuster of the AJC, was making his first visit to Israel.

---

[325] William Zukerman, *Voice of Dissent: Jewish Problems 1948-1961*, page 139-140.
[326] Harry Greenstein, "Notes on Israel," mimeograph, Heidelberg, June 1949. Approximately 60 pages, page 2, AJC library.
[327] Harry Greenstein, "Mission to Israel, October 15 to October 29, 1949," mimeograph, 33 pages, page 8, "Tour of Agricultural Settlements," file A-2-10 "AJC FILE NO. 3 1950(continued)," JHU.

Two months after statehood was declared, Joseph Proskauer did suggest to Arthur Lourie, Israel's representative in New York — in an interestingly tentative way — that the welfare of Arab residents of Palestine might well require slowing Jewish immigration. This ironically echoed the "absorptive capacity" policy of the British Mandatory which had drawn organized Jewish outrage:

> *I hope you will not think it heresy if I say that we should give careful attention to the argument that the economic unity envisaged by the partition resolution necessarily involved some consideration of the effect of utterly unrestricted immigration on the Arab economy.*
>
> *I pose merely for consideration of those who have the responsibility of decision the thought that ultimate uncontrolled immigration may have to come in several stages rather than in one initial stage.*
>
> *I wish to make very clear to you that the thoughts I am here expressing are, for the time being at least, submitted for the consideration of your Government. I venture to suggest that you send a copy of this letter to Epstein, with my assurance to him that I shall be glad to cooperate with him within the limits of the obligations of myself and my associates as American citizens.* [328]

A few days previously, Lourie had relayed a cable to Proskauer from Israeli Foreign Minister Moshe Shertok [Sharett], which was much less tentative in suggesting desirable US policy:

> *I was happy to hear from Arthur Lourie of your keen and continuing interest in Israel's fortunes of which I was confident. I believe that the present emergency offers an opportunity for the effective reopening of the embargo question, also for urging that the full weight and authority of the United States government be maintained behind proposals for an international regime in Jerusalem..... I feel sure that you will keep in touch with Epstein* [Elath, ambassador in Washington] *regarding any efforts you may yourself be able to undertake.*[329]

In October 1950 there was an interesting dialog that Blaustein had with assistant secretary of state McGhee about the return of Arab

---

[328] Proskauer to Arthur Lourie, Provisional Government of Israel, NY, July 15, 1948, Box 2.21, file C-2-23 Proskauer, Judge Joseph M. JHU.
[329] Lourie to Proskauer, July 12, 1948, *ibid.*

refugees:

> McGhee said he thought that something would really have to be done about the Arab refugee situation before the Arabs would agree to peace.
> JB said that as a matter of fact at McGhee's suggestion, JB was helpful in getting the Israel government sometime ago to agree to taking back 100,000 Arab Jews (sic) but that the Arab countries would not go through with it and that now JB did not see how Israel could possibly take back any large number, if any, of Arab refugees for two reasons: (1) because of the question of loyalty and (2) because of no way to handle them in the Israeli economy.
> McGhee said he thought he could see why the Arab refugees could not be brought back to the towns, but he thought they could be placed in the rural areas where perhaps they had lived.
> JB asked McGhee if he had been to Israel and McGhee said no. JB said that if McGhee had been there he would see that this latest thought of his is impracticable, and that as a matter of fact, these rural settlements are now occupied by Jewish immigrants and that, as McGhee knows, they are still living in camps and tents.[330]

In the conference, as he had done with Truman the previous month,[331] Jacob promoted the idea of Israel as a military ally in the containment of the Soviet Union, and urged US support of Jewish immigration to Israel to strengthen the military manpower of Israel, bolstering its ability to fight alongside the United States and its allies in case of war with Russia.

---

[330] "MEMO JB Conference with McGhee, Berry & Rockwell (Washington), October 17, 1950," page 6, Box 1.56, folder 991 "McGhee Asst. Secretary of State 1949-1950," JHU. The map on page 92 shows Jewish settlement at the time of Partition. The task undertaken by the new government after the 1949 armistice was to establish Jewish presence in Arab-evacuated areas of the new State. Jewish immigrants were settled in available housing and tent communities as quickly as possible. Populating the Galilee and Negev by Jews is still a political priority. Jewish settlement in occupied West Bank (Judea and Samaria), Gaza and the Sinai followed the 1967 war.
[331] See page 173.

The AJC vs the ACJ

FOLLOWING THE declaration of Israeli statehood in May 1948, Blaustein and the AJC "ran interference" against public American Jewish expressions of anti-Zionism, led by the American Council for Judaism(ACJ).

The American Council for Judaism began with a statement issued by a meeting of self-proclaimed "Non-Zionist Rabbis" in Atlantic City in June 1942, declaring,
> We, Rabbis in American Israel, who believe in the universalism of Judaism's ethical and spiritual values and teachings, express our hearty agreement with the following Statement...
> We believe that the present tragic experience of mankind abundantly demonstrate(s) that no single people or group can hope to live in freedom and security when their neighbors are in the grip of evil forces either as perpetrators or sufferers. We hold, therefore, that the solution of the social, economic, and political problems of one people is inextricably bound up with those of others...
> We declare our unwavering faith in the humane and righteous principles that underlie the democratic way of life, principles first envisaged by the Prophets of Israel and embodied in our American Bill of Rights....
> Realizing how dear Palestine is to the Jewish soul...we stand ready to render unstinted aid to our brethren in their economic, cultural and spiritual endeavors in that country. But in the light of our universalistic interpretation of Jewish history and destiny, and also because of our concern for the welfare and status of the Jewish people living in other parts of the world, we are unable to subscribe to or support the political emphasis now paramount in the Zionist program.[332]

The Council's Alfred Lilienthal wrote a 1949 *Reader's Digest* article, "Israel's Flag is Not Mine," and followed it with the book *What Price Israel*(1953) and others. The Council's Elmer Berger, a Flint, Michigan, rabbi, in 1942 began a campaign to counter Zionism in American Judaism. He was indefatigable in what became lifelong work for the idea of "Jews as emancipated and integrated citizens of the countries in which

---
[332]"Statement of Principles Atlantic City June 1942," Isadore Breslau Papers; P-507; box 2; folder 16; AJHS.

they live and hope to live" (p. viii, Berger, *The Jewish Dilemma*, 1945) and to distinguish between *Judaism or Jewish Nationalism*, to cite the title of his 1957 book.

Feeling beset by "improper" publicity by Israel and her advocates, and by the American Council for Judaism, a front-page article in November 1949 in the Committee newsletter read,

Jewish Organizations Urged to Halt Open Controversy in Public Press

Meeting in Chicago the weekend of Oct. 22-23, the AJC executive committee urged Jewish organizations to refrain from engaging in open controversy in the public press because of the harm they do to the position of Jews in the United States...

The sessions, attended by more than 100 members of the executive group and chapter representatives from 28 major communities, were devoted largely to the problems created by statements from Zionist and anti-Zionist groups giving the American public the impression that Israel is intervening in the internal affairs of American Jews and impugning their patriotism and loyalty.

In preparation for this meeting AJC chapter officials studied pertinent background material...This material included excerpts from a statement reportedly made by Prime Minister Ben Gurion to an American Histadrut delegation in Israel last August, together with a letter from Jacob Blaustein, AJC president, to the Israeli Prime Minister on the Committee's reaction to that statement, and excerpts from the Council for Judaism endorsed article by Alfred M. Lilienthal in the September Readers Digest.

To provide a comprehensive basis for the delegates deliberations, Mr. Blaustein made a presentation covering all facets of the problem. He referred not only to the remarks attributed to Mr. Ben Gurion, but to the statements of American Zionists, especially one by Daniel Frisch, ZOA president, on Aug. 20,[333] and to the steps

---

[333]The *New York Times* reported,
> Mr. Frisch called for a "thorough revision of the of both the aims and methods of Hebrew education in America. ...We must fearlessly think through the whole purpose of Jewish education in America in relation to our own mode of life as Jews and to the State of Israel."

"Israel Reassured on Influx of Arabs," *New York Times*, August 22, 1949, page 10.

taken by the AJC in recent weeks. These included cables to the Israeli Prime Minister and to the Foreign Minister, correspondence and conferences with Israeli emissaries in this country and an informal meeting with a number of leading American Zionists.

In these conferences and communications, Mr. Blaustein reported, the historic opposition of the AJC to the concept of world Jewish nationalism was strongly reasserted.

Similarly, with regard to the Council, Mr. Blaustein referred not only to the Lilienthal article, but to various releases and publicity based, among other things, on addresses to its chapter by prominent non-Jews. He charged such publicity is harmful and self-defeating.

In the discussion which followed, the delegates reaffirmed the AJC position that it is axiomatic that American Jews, "while having an abiding friendship for the new state and a sincere desire as Americans to aid in its development, have no political affiliation with the State of Israel," and emphasized their unalterable opposition to any concept of world Jewish nationalism.

....During the discussions devoted to the Council's publicity, the intense reactions caused within the Jewish community and its usage by professional anti-Semites were cited. There was an overwhelming consensus that this publicity had the effect of unwarrantedly impugning the loyalty and patriotism of American Jews in the eyes of their fellow citizens and threatened the Jewish position in this country.

Herbert B. Ehrmann, of Boston, AJC vice president, presented a plan for an educational program... Briefly, the AJC holds that American Jews consider that in every way their future is in the US... and that neither segregation, on the one hand, nor abandonment of Jewish ties, on the other, is necessary or desirable...

The AJC has begun to produce materials setting forth these themes, citing the factual realities at their base, which will be used intensively in a program of informal adult education.[334]

(The main topic of the article was that Frisch said Assistant Secretary of State George McGhee told him Israel would not be required by the United States to accept large numbers of returning Arab refugees, or cede any of the Negev. See page 195.)
[334] *Committee Reporter*, Vol. 6 No. 11, November 1949, AJC.

Jacob wrote to Council president Lessing Rosenwald, March 17, 1950, that they shared a "mutual abhorrence for world Jewish political nationalism." The letter then repeats the AJC insistence that Council criticisms of Israeli and American Zionists be confined to the "Yiddish and Anglo-Jewish" press.

> We do not consider trifling the citations furnished to you of Council publicity being used by anti-Semites....What counts is the fact that the line taken by the Council, even though of different intent, has been virtually indistinguishable from the line taken by the professional anti-Semites. Whether they follow the Council, or whether the Council follows them, is immaterial.

The letter warned that anti-Semites would use American Council for Judaism publicity material. "Their propaganda is made more insidious by reason of the fact that they are able to claim that some Jews agree with them."[335]

The Jewish Telegraphic Agency (JTA) reported of AJC President Emeritus Proskauer, "Speaking at an American Jewish Committee luncheon at Hotel Martinique, he expressed astonishment at the negative attitude of one extremist group towards Israel."[336]

In 1957, *Time* magazine wrote, "Of all the painful thorns in their international rosebush, none makes Israelis so sore as a group of highly vocal American Jews known as the American Council for Judaism, Inc." Lessing J. Rosenwald is quoted saying of the Israelis, "To them, Jews who are in other parts of the world and who are in difficulty should receive no assistance other than to help them come to Israel—all else is temporizing. It is difficult for them to conceive how a Jew can live a normal life, be free and independent, outside of Israel. I do not think they can understand how I, a Jew, can love the United States as they do Israel. They cannot understand a Jew integrating himself into the fabric of any nation other than Israel."

The article concludes, "Proof that Israel has in the U.S. more roses than thorns lay in Miami Beach, where some 2,000 U.S. and Canadian Jews gathered last week to kick off the 1957 Israel bond drive. The goal: $75 million."[337]

---

[335] Blaustein to Rosenwald, March 17, 1950. Box 2.21, file C-2-31, Rosenwald, Lessing 1950, JHU.
[336] "Proskauer Criticizes Groups Holding Extremist Views on Stand of U.S. Jews to Israel," JTA News, May 12, 1950, page 4, Box 2.21, file C-2-23 Proskauer, Judge Joseph M., JHU
[337] "Opinion: Jews vs. Israel," Time, Feb. 25, 1957.

In 1957, Rosenwald made his first visit to Israel, and the New York Times reported:
> He also criticized what he called the indifference on the part of Israelis to the plight of Arab refugees. "While Israel obtained from Germany reparations for expropriated property," he said, "I wonder what its attitude will be when it comes to make recompense to the 'displaced' Arabs. Surely the two cases are not too dissimilar."[338]

Rosenwald was an excellent example of a supporter of a Jewish home in Palestine who nonetheless disdained crude nationalism. He was a participant in the Feb. 17, 1924 Non-Partisan Conference for Palestine.[339]

In 1957 the AJC issued a 20-page booklet, "demonstrating that Council propaganda was used by anti-Semites to bolster hostile attitudes toward Jews."[340] The publication's passages defined the results the Committee felt the Council should fear, of aiming at Zionists but damaging the place of Jews in America:
> The Council spokesmen say they are not anti-Israel or pro-Israel; they are not anti-Arab or pro-Arab; they are pro-American....
> In other words, they say that the attack is on American Zionists only, not on Israel. But, as already pointed out, "Zionist" in the minds of Americans can and does denote a vast alignment -- all who work in the interest of Israel, those who give and those who exert efforts in its behalf. This might include as much as 90 per cent of American Jews today.[341]

338"Critic Unswayed by Visit to Israel," Feb. 14, 1957, *New York Times*, page 7.
339"PALESTINE Non-Partisan Conference 1924," General Correspondence 1906-1932, Box 16, AJC.
340*In Vigilant Brotherhood*, AJC, 1964.
341*The Nature and Consequences of the Public Relations Activities of the American Council for Judaism*, American Jewish Committee, 1957, page 10.

Index

Acheson, Dean..........143, 146n, 147

Adler, Cyrus....51, 55, 59n, 60, 61n, 68, 73, 76

AJC Executive Committee... 24, 59, 60, 61, 67, 68, 69, 70n, 95, 96, 98, 101n, 104n, 117, 118, 119, 120n, 162n, 180, 201

Allen, George V. 142

American Council for Judaism (ACJ) 10n, 12, 52, 99, 117, 158, 181, 200, 201, 203, 204

Arendt, Hannah...........................8

Austin, Warren..................136, 168

B'not Yaakov.........................15, 161

Ben-Gurion, David...1, 5, 6, 11, 125, 136, 144, 146, 147, 178, 179, 180, 182, 184, 185, 186, 188, 189, 201

Berger, Elmer 51, 77, 123, 159, 200, 201

Bernadotte, Count Folke....152, 153

Bernheim, I.W. 51, 67, 68

Bevin, Earnest...........................119

Brandeis, Louis D. .. 51, 60, 61n, 85, 89, 105, 109, 110

Breslau, Isadore.................109, 124

Byroade, Henry A. 141, 142, 144, 145, 146, 147, 169, 170, 171, 172

Chesterton, G.K. 87

Churchill, Winston S. 85

CIA...................6n, 108, 111, 136

Cohen, Elliot E. 126, 158

Commentary Magazine..... 105, 106

Communism..15, 128, 166, 169, 173

Diaspora 4n, 5, 11, 15, 16n, 58n, 89, 108, 113, 130, 133, 184, 188n, 190

Dulles, John Foster....142, 143, 146

Eban, Aubrey S. (Abba)....105, 106, 143, 146, 161, 164, 182

Einstein, Albert..............................8

Elath (Epstein), Eliahu...........143n, 150n, 178-182, 195, 198

Federation of American Zionists 54, 59, 60

Glueck, Nelson...................104, 105

Goldmann, Nahum 9n, 12, 95, 101, 182

Greenstein, Harry.......................197

Haganah...............................43, 44

Harman, Avraham......................167

Herzl, Theodor.....64n, 81, 87, 93n, 113, 122, 124, 185

Hilldring, John H. 143n, 152

Hook, Sidney..........................8, 191

Irgun.......................6, 7, 8, 115, 134

Jerusalem 1, 4, 38, 53, 54, 55, 105, 134, 135, 151, 152, 162, 165, 166, 190, 195, 196, 198

Jewish Agency..5, 12, 15, 21, 23, 24, 45, 73, 76, 77, 94, 95, 96, 98, 99, 102, 104, 108, 114, 115, 116, 117, 118, 119, 120, 125, 134, 135, 143n, 178, 188, 193

Kohn, Hans................ 103, 104, 105

Layton, Irving............................124

Lazaron, Rabbi Morris S. 2, 192

Lichtblau, Nathan................156, 157

Lilienthal, Alfred M. ..12, 200, 201, 202
Lipsky, Louis..............59, 60, 65, 76
Lourie, Arthur............................198
Lowenberg, Helmut....134, 135, 136
Magnes, Judah L. 51, 54, 60, 61, 68, 96, 105, 106, 114
Marshall, George C. ..13n, 154, 155
Marshall, Louis 10n, 14n, 51, 55, 61, 63, 67, 70, 73, 76, 77n, 80, 83
Marshall Plan..............169, 176, 194
Meir (Myerson), Golda. .1, 184, 188
Morrison-Grady Plan(1946).....136, 137
Operation Susannah..........170, 188
Peel Plan (1937)...................90, 101
Philipson, Rev. David 66, 83-84
Proskauer, Joseph......1, 5, 9, 11, 24, 45, 59n, 77, 93, 94, 95, 96, 101, 113, 114, 115, 117, 118, 120, 121, 129, 131, 150, 152, 178, 179, 180, 182, 190, 198, 203
Qibya (Kibya) Massacre. 11, 15, 145, 146, 161, 162, 164, 165
Roosevelt, Franklin D. ...21, 93, 94, 110, 141, 156
Rosenwald, Lessing. .10n, 178, 180, 203, 204
Ruppin, Arthur..............54, 55, 98n
Segal, Simon....143, 151n, 158, 159, 161, 164, 182, 193, 197
Sharett (Shertok), Moshe....11, 144, 145, 150, 158, 168, 180, 182, 198
Silver, Abba Hillel......93n, 96, 124, 125, 178n
Slawson, John.......99, 114, 150, 167

Sokolow, Nahum.................80, 86n
State Department....6, 54, 101, 142, 143, 145n, 149, 152, 164, 165, 169, 173, 195
Stern Gang.......9, 115, 134, 135, 152
Stern, Horace M. 73, 74, 130
Stone, Dewey...................... 153, 155
Stone, I.F. 110
Straus, Nathan............................54
Stroock, Allen M. 10n, 132n
Szold, Henrietta.................2, 57, 58
Terrorism......7, 8, 9, 24, 25, 37, 38, 115, 126, 134, 135, 152
Truman, Harry S. .. 21, 93, 115, 121, 142, 143, 147, 149-157, 173, 174, 177, 193, 199
Waldman, Morris D. 109, 122n, 133, 182, 192
Weisbord, Albert.........................85
Weizmann, Chaim....38, 69, 74-78, 80, 109, 110, 114, 132, 144, 173, 177, 182
Weizmann-Stroock Conferences (1941-42)...........132, 182
White Paper(1939)...22, 29, 34, 94, 118
Wise, Stephen S. ...59, 63, 123, 124, 129
Yishuv..........6, 76, 97, 110, 134-137
World Zionist Organization (WZO) ..5, 11n, 16n, 45, 52, 65, 68, 73-77, 80, 94, 101, 178
Zionist Organization of America (ZOA) 45, 54, 59-60, 83, 94, 111, 127, 128, 178, 201
Zukerman, William....................196